THE COACHING AGE

THE COACHING AGE

DAVID MOUNTFIELD

ROBERT HALE & COMPANY

ISBN 0 7091 5258 2

Robert Hale & Company
Clerkenwell House
Clerkenwell Green
London EC1R 0HT

Filmset by Specialised Offset Services Ltd, Liverpool
and printed and bound in Great Britain by
Redwood Burn Limited, Trowbridge and Esher

CONTENTS

AUTHOR'S NOTE

Grateful thanks are due to many people who helped in the writing of this book, especially to John Copeland, who very kindly read the manuscript.

ILLUSTRATIONS

PICTURE CREDITS

By Gracious Permission of Her Majesty the Queen, 24; Mansell Collection, 1, 5, 41, 43; Radio Times Hulton Picture Library, 2, 7, 10, 12, 21, 29, 32, 33, 34, 36; Science Museum, 3, 6, 18, 19, 37, 38, 42; Barnaby's Picture Library, 8; London Museum, 9; Post Office, 13, 14, 15, 16; National Portrait Gallery, 17; Powell Collection, 39.

ONE

Introduction

The stage-coach: it is hard to think of any image that summons more readily a romantic notion of some long-lost Merrie England – a place of exquisite fashions and elegant spas, of vigorous sport and splendid horses, of huge debts and sly courtships, of mighty sirloins and sparkling decanters. No wonder coaching prints are so popular with manufacturers of Christmas cards – for there is always a coach on the mantelpiece along with the robin, the holly and the still-life painted with the mouth. This is not merely modern fancy, nor the legacy of Mr Pickwick. The coach was always associated with Christmas, perhaps because it was the coach that first permitted scattered friends and families to gather for the Christmas holiday.

It is a white Christmas of course: a trace of snow on roofs and branches, or a road glittering with frost and echoing the clipped hoofbeats of the smartly trotting horses. The coach itself is decked with holly, its trim lines and bright paint almost hidden by the luggage piled high on the roof. A goose is strapped to the railing, hampers are tucked under feet and, perched on top, there is always an old lady's canary in its cage. The coachman, with his double-thonged whip, holds the reins easily in his left hand, the lightness of his touch contrasting with the immense bulk of his caped and coated form. From among the beaver hats of the outside passengers, the guard rises to blow a blast on his horn, a note of warning to other traffic, a note of advice to those waiting on the road ahead, and a note of congratulation to himself and the passengers on their splendid situation. The horn blows, the red wheels spin, a barking dog runs close behind. Not far along the road, an inn prepares a mellow welcome.

They were "jolly times", sighed an old coachman reminiscently as he sat in the bar of the Railway Hotel, clasping his glass with fingers permanently bent by long hours gripping the reins. And, "What is more delightful", inquired the Eighth Duke of Beaufort, whose position in life enabled him to indulge as a hobby what the old coachman could no longer follow as a profession, "What is more delightful than a good and picturesque road, a well-built and well-running carriage, harness properly fitted, horses bitted and put-to so that they go with ease to themselves . . ."

What was more delightful than to escape from London, grimier in 1830 than now, on a summer afternoon, and find oneself in a few minutes rattling along a road between hedgerows bright with wildflowers, with the green fields stretching beyond, the sky innocent of aircraft, and the road free of jams – except the occasional flock of sheep. And what a tremendous speed is ten miles an hour when travelling on top of a coach.

The traveller is always in touch with the passing scenery, taking a glass at the inn while the horses are changed, raising his hat to a passing pedestrian, jumping down to walk while the coach climbs a hill. He is not whisked from place to place, forlornly watching the countryside slip by beyond a smoky pane. There is time to exchange gossip with an innkeeper, to buy a cheese from a farmer, to have a shave or buy a bonnet.

"Perhaps", said Colonel Corbett, who in his day had driven many a mile four-in-hand through the mountains of Wales, "there is not time for such a mode of travelling now . . . but, as a nearly worn-out old roadster, it strikes me there may be too much haste for comfort."

What value is there in the nostalgic recollections of the old coachmen? Is the Christmas-card image a true one? There is certainly another side to the story. For some people, a coach journey was the nastiest experience imaginable.

Rising in pitch darkness at four or five o'clock in the morning, groping a way through the ill-lit streets to the coach office, pestered by insolent and importunate porters, squeezed into a stuffy wooden box with ill-smelling strangers, jolted and rattled hour after hour in constant fear of overturning in the ditch, ejected at an inn where the food is served so hot that it cannot be eaten in the time allowed by the timetable (one traveller hid the spoons in the teapot to gain a few minutes while the host howled "Thieves!") delayed by storms, breakdowns, tollgates or runaway horses, frozen stiff in winter, baked to a sweat in summer – no one could say it was the perfect way to travel. It was also, by railway standards, very slow and very expensive: the early railways cut both journey times and fares by about three-quarters.

Coaching could never be a means of mass transportation like the railways. The fare from London to Edinburgh would have cost a working man several months' wages, and only a small proportion of the population could afford to travel often by coach. Yet the coach was not the exclusively middle-class convenience it is often said to have been. Except for the poorest labouring classes, who in the early nineteenth century were excluded from virtually every social activity except work, people of all sorts travelled – occasionally – by coach.

Passenger transport in Britain in the early nineteenth century provides a good illustration of the principle that, in the industrial revolution, major technological change was preceded by the rapid development of traditional methods, to a point at which demand exceeded capacity. The great age of coaching was short. It began after the end of the Napoleonic wars and reached a peak in the 1820s and 1830s. By 1840, coaching was disintegrating under pressure from the swiftly spreading railways. The coach could no more compete with the locomotive than the weaver could compete with the power loom.

In its brief span of glory, coaching in Britain attained a high degree of efficiency. The speed and regularity of the long-distance mails and the fast day-coaches would have seemed incredible to people living a generation or two earlier and, indeed, struck contemporaries with amazement. Foreign visitors were filled with admiration and envy. But, in a few short years, it was all over. The railways made a mockery of the times recorded and the numbers carried by the coaches, and in next to no time the coach had been degraded to a rich man's plaything or a quaint reminder of 'days of yore'. People soon forgot that, *before* the railways, Britain had enjoyed the finest public-transport system the world had ever seen. Bemused by the transformation wrought by iron and coal, social historians neglected the more modest transformation effected by the coach and four horses. To this day, by comparison with the enormous flood of books, popular and scholarly, on the development of railways and (somewhat less) of canals, books on coaching hardly amount to a trickle – merely a sporadic drip. Moreover, most books about coaching (including this one) tend to rely largely on a few rather well-thumbed sources; scholarly research on the subject does not, apparently, enjoy great support.

The origin of the word 'coach' has been disputed since the early seventeenth century. Jacques Damase believes it is of Celtic origin, but the most widely held opinion, in the seventeenth century and since, is that the word derives, by a roundabout route, from a village west of Budapest known as Kocs (pronounced 'cosh'), on the old road to Vienna. Presumably, it was one of many halts on that well-travelled road, and why it should have given its name to the light-weight carriages that ran between the two capitals in the late fifteenth century is a mystery; possibly, the local carriagebuilders were noted for special skill.

Of course, wheeled vehicles drawn by animals were used in prehistoric societies and are perhaps almost as old as the wheel itself (an old German history of the carriage began with the Garden of Eden). The coach was distinguished from earlier vehicles by two characteristics: it had a roof which was an integral part of the structure, and it was in some way sprung or suspended to ameliorate the jolting of the wheels. This definition, neat enough in theory, is less useful in practice, for the word was used indiscriminately in the sixteenth and seventeenth centuries to describe any reasonably elaborate carriage, regardless of its suspension. Early references to coaches cannot, therefore, be taken literally, and the typical fifteenth-century Hungarian vehicle was not a true coach, having no suspension nor a fixed roof. In fact the nature of any vehicle is not always clear from fifteenth- and sixteenth-century descriptions.

One of the earliest references to what seems to have been a genuine coach concerns the vehicle given to the king of France by the king of Hungary in 1457. It is said to have been *branlant*, 'shaking', an effect that may have been created by leather slings holding the body between four posts. But it must have made an unfavourable impression, for nearly one hundred years later there were still only three coaches in the whole of Paris. On the evidence of the chronicler Stow, the first coach to be made in England was made by Walter Rippon for the Earl of Rutland in 1555. True or not (there are other claimants), the history of the true coach in England begins in the second half of the sixteenth century.

Although the introduction of a form of suspension was obviously a considerable advance, there is no sound technological reason why coaches should not have been invented hundreds of years earlier (archaeological evidence suggests that a form of suspension was used in certain Roman carriages). That they were not argues that there was no great need for them, and this view is supported by the very slow growth of coaching. There were no public stage-coaches until the reign of Charles I, and very few before about the middle of the eighteenth century. The coach did not reach the height of its development until about 1820–30 – and the Stockton-Darlington railway opened in 1825.

TWO

Miry Ways

The fundamental reason for the slow growth of coaching can be stated in a word – roads – or rather, the badness of roads. Not until the days of Telford and McAdam was the technique of road-building and maintenance generally appreciated, just in time to give the coaches their brief but glorious Indian summer before the railways put them out of business.

As everyone knows, the Romans were the first serious road-builders in Europe. Their roads were soundly based and meant to last as long as the Roman empire – for ever, in fact. They did outlast the empire, and were incorporated in bits in the modern road system, but they were intended to move soldiers swiftly between base and frontier, and were not designed to assist the population at large. They were straight, though not quite so straight as is often assumed (being practical men, the Romans did not invariably choose to go over an obstacle rather than round it) but they did not necessarily follow trade routes or link centres of population.

Although the old Roman roads remained in use in many places, medieval Europe had no need of great 'throughways'. The decline of towns and the proliferation of frontiers equally discouraged road building and, from the scanty evidence available, it seems that medieval roads, such as they were, on the whole fulfilled the needs of medieval society. At any rate, they were less unsatisfactory than they became in the sixteenth and seventeenth centuries.

The decline probably began in the fourteenth century as part of the general economic recession associated with the interruption of the growth of population which has been observed early in the fourteenth century and was exacerbated by recurrent plague as well as, perhaps, the persistence of war. In the fifteenth century, says Paul Murray Kendall, "the average road was a country lane running through deep woods and across sweeps of moor and marsh, un-signposted, generating forks and branching tracks to puzzle the traveller, sometimes ending abruptly at a ford that had disappeared under high water".* But the situation did not become really serious in England until the sixteenth century, when expanding population and trade – and therefore traffic – caused rapid deterioration and a rising tide of complaint. One result was the Highways Act of 1555.

This was the first government act that attempted to introduce a national system of road maintenance, and in spite of the fact that the system it imposed proved far from adequate, it remained the basis of administration until the General Highways Act of 1835. Some of its provisions were still in force when Henry Ford set up his first workshop in Detroit.

The act confirmed that the maintenance of the roads should be the responsibility of local authorities, in this case the parish councils. Every householder had to provide labour for roadworks, later commuted in some cases to a cash payment. A Surveyor of the Highways was to be appointed in each parish, and it was upon this reluctant (and unpaid) official that the chief burden fell. Among his numerous duties, he had to inspect all the roads and bridges in his area, ensure that the various landlords carried out their responsibilities where their land adjoined the highway, watch out for illegal vehicles (such as wagons drawn by more than the number of horses laid down by statute), make regular reports to the justices of the Highway Sessions, and persuade the justices to levy a rate sufficient to pay for his expenses. Worst of all, he was responsible for seeing that his fellow citizens carried out their duties in repairing, clearing or rebuilding the roads. During the year he held office, the Surveyor was one of the most unpopular people in the parish.

To us children of the motor age, a 'road' is a smooth strip of hard material laid across country between narrow and constant limits, and serving a single function – the transport of vehicles.

---

*The Yorkist Age 1962.

Such a conception would have been entirely foreign in Tudor England. A 'road' then was little more than a right of way, almost an idea rather than an object, a matter of simple convenience to avoid unnecessary damage to crops. There were no strict limits confining the road between verges; indeed, there were often no verges, and if the road were in so bad a condition that the traveller could not easily pass, he was entitled to take to the fields on either side, "for avoydance of the Miry ways", as a seventeenth-century preacher explained. As a result, it was sometimes impossible to tell where the 'road' (in the modern sense) ran at all. To follow the advice of Jeremiah – "Stand ye in the ways, and see, and ask for the old paths, where is the good way, and walk therein" – was hardly possible. A traveller who approached a town from the south one year might find himself approaching it from the east a year later. It was reported in the early eighteenth century that two coaches crossing Thetford Heath passed each other a mile apart. Some towns rang a bell to guide visitors through the surrounding wilderness, and some placed a light in the church tower after dark to indicate their whereabouts. Signposts were rarely found; an act of the 1690s that enforced the duty of erecting signposts at crossroads on the parishes seems to have been generally ignored with impunity.

Many people were unwilling to concede that the roads should be exclusively reserved for travel. The borough of Coventry found it necessary in the fifteenth century to pass a law saying "that no man from henceforth dig clay . . . in the highway betwixt Summerleaze Butts and Spoon market, upon pain of 40d". As late as the eighteenth century, a Nottinghamshire man was prosecuted for causing an obstruction in the road "whereof the King's subjects . . . could not pass". He had been digging for coal.

Even if the technique and the cash necessary for building concrete or tarmac roads had been available, such roads would not have been built because the traffic did not demand them. A horse does not require a level, hard surface, still less an ox (the more common draught animal in hilly districts). A wheeled vehicle, on the other hand, runs more easily on a hard, dry road, and the differing requirements of rider and driver were often the cause of angry disputes.

However, until the sixteenth century, and in many areas much later, wheeled vehicles were comparatively rare in the British Isles. Most Scotsmen and all Highlanders never saw so much as a farm cart before the eighteenth century. Northumberland had "not a cart in the country" in 1749. The general method of transport, for passengers as well as goods, was the back of a horse. Heavy goods went as far as possible by water: the usual route from Norwich to London, for instance, was down the Wensum and the Yare to Yarmouth., along the coast and up the Thames. But even the most inconvenient loads, such as building stone, were stometimes transported by packhorse.

Long trains of packhorses, thirty or forty together, were still a common sight in some parts of England in the mid eighteenth century. They were often preferred to carts and wagons even when vehicles were available – more evidence of the poor state of the roads. Packhorses were invariably quicker than carts, largely because they did not get stuck so easily, and they were sometimes cheaper.

In south-eastern England, except for large parts of Sussex, wagons were fairly common by the accession of Elizabeth. But, traditionally, they were summer vehicles; with the rains of autumn every year, wagons were packed away in barns to await the spring. One advantage of the wagon over the packhorse was that fragile goods could be better protected from mishap or rough weather. England's most valuable product – wool – had usually been carried by packhorse, but the growth of the cloth trade in the sixteenth century led to increasing use of wagons. Moreover, the traffic was less and less confined to the summer months. The effect on the already deteriorating roads was dire.

On unmade-up surfaces, wagons cause infinitely greater damage than horses. Quite a number of horses can plod along the same path without necessarily treading in each other's footsteps. Their hooves may chop up the surface somewhat, but the effect is nothing compared to a loaded wagon, which is not only far heavier but also has a relatively smaller area in contact with the surface and makes continuous ruts. The expression 'cut to ribbons' can be applied almost literally to a sixteenth-century road subjected to heavy wagon traffic after a spell of wet weather.

Various efforts were made, without much success, to prevent this kind of damage. A royal proclamation of 1622 forbade the use of wagons altogether for transporting goods; only two-wheeled carts were permitted. This draconian measure was short-lived, and probably disobeyed rather widely during the few years it remained in force. In 1670, wagons drawn by eight horses were permitted – strictness giving way to permissiveness. An act of 1763 attempted to outlaw wagon wheels less than nine inches wide at the rim, later restricted to eight-horse wagons. Tolls were levied on a sliding scale – the wider the wheel, the smaller the toll. An act of 1822 forbade wheels less than three inches wide on any wagon, but it aroused such protest that it had to be repealed.

Wide wheels may have been better for the roads but, as every carrier knew, they made the wagon less manoeuvrable and, through greater friction, harder to pull. Many clever devices were adopted to improve performance or, alternatively, evade the law. In wet and hilly districts, wheels were not only narrow but sometimes fitted with iron studs, which ripped up the surface as effectively as a plough. The regulations against narrow wheels were avoided by fitting a narrow band around the circumference so that the wheel did not rest on the full width of its rim, or by bevelling the edges. Wide wheels, it was thought, ought to improve the surface by rolling it, and an invention of 1763 capitalized on this notion with a front axle much shorter than the rear, so that the wide wheels actually 'rolled' a strip five feet wide. But whatever the effect on the road, this contrivance was too difficult for horses to haul.

The condition of the English roads can only be gauged from the comments of discontented travellers. A gentleman cashing in on the Dissolution of the Monasteries (1536) grumbled that "lead from the roofs cannot be conveyed away 'till next summer, for the ways . . . are so foule and deepe that no carriage can pass in winter". The disappearance of the monasteries in fact added to the deterioration, for the monks were among the few who by and large maintained the roads on their lands. William Harrison, author of an Elizabethan guide to England, admitted reluctantly in 1586: "Now to speake generallie of our common high waies . . . you shall understand that in the claie or cledgie soile they are often verie deepe and troublesome in the winter halfe". At the end of the reign, a morris dancer on his way from London to Norwich found progress difficult and sometimes dangerous:

"At length coming to a broad plash of water and mud, which could not be avoided, I fetched a rise, yet fell in over the ankles at the further end. My youth that followed me took his jump, and stuck fast in the midst".

The following century brought little improvement. Ralph Thoresby, the much-travelled diarist of the seventeenth century, recorded what Macaulay describes as "such a series of perils and disasters as might suffice for a journey to the Frozen Ocean or to the Desert of Sahara". In spite of legislation and the introduction of the turnpike system, no really substantial improvement seems to have taken place before about the middle of the eighteenth century. On his tour through Great Britain in the 1720s, Defoe found that Harrison's warning about "claie or cledgie soile" in the Midlands was still applicable: "the great number of horses every year kill'd by the excess of labour in those heavy ways, has been such a charge to the country, that new building of causeways, as the Romans did of old, seems to me to be a much easier expense".

By the mid eighteenth century, the roads around London for a distance of twenty or thirty miles are said to have been good, yet according to Lord Hervey it was impossible to get from Kensington up to town in 1736: "The road between this place and London is grown so infamously bad that we live here in the same solitude as if cast on a rock in the middle of the ocean. All Londoners tell us that between us and them is an impassable gulf of mud". There were three possible routes into town but all of them were unsatisfactory: of the two roads through the park, said Lord Hervey in 1743, the new one was "so convex and the old one so concave that by this extreme of faults they agree in the common one of being, like the highroad, impassable".

Within the city itself, conditions were sometimes little better. When George II went to open Parliament in 1759, the ruts in the road had to be filled up before his coach could pass.

In the rest of the country there were still large areas where the roads were virtually non-existent. Throughout Lancashire and most of north-west England, the best that the traveller could hope for was a narrow cobbled path, two or three feet wide, raised above the valley of mud that was the 'road'. "Travellers who encountered each other on these elevated causeways sometimes tried to wear out each other's patience rather than either would risk a diversion", wrote the Webbs, for having once descended into the morass, the horseman had a terrific struggle to get back on the path. The Great North Road all the way north of Grantham was of this type as late as 1739. Below the causeway, the road might have sunk ten feet or more: stags, pursued by hounds and huntsmen, were said to have frequently leapt over a loaded wagon whose top barely reached the level of the fields.

The state of the roads made travel not only difficult but dangerous. Apart from the ordinary effects of falling from a horse when it stumbled in a rut, people could be – and were – drowned in a hole. An Ipswich newspaper in 1769 reported an inquest on a man who had been thrown from his horse and "suffocated by mud and filth".

One of the fiercest critics of the roads in the eighteenth century was Arthur Young, whose attitude was complicated by contradictory resentments. While appreciating the importance of road improvement for trade, he regretted the drift of population from the countryside to London and other large cities which was encouraged by easier travel. This ambiguity perhaps led him into an exaggerated condemnation of road conditions. Writing in 1770, he remarked of a road in Lancashire: "I know not in the whole range of language terms sufficiently expressive to describe this infernal road. Travellers will here meet with ruts which I actually measured, four feet deep, and floating with mud only from a wet summer. What, therefore, must it be after a winter? The only mending it receives is tumbling in some loose stones which serve no other purpose than jolting the carriage in the most intolerable manner". The West Country was no better; there the roads were "mere rocky lanes full of hugeous stones as big as one's horse, and abominable holes". The irate traveller could hardly believe that he was on the main road to Cardiff, in spite of assurances from the local inhabitants, of whom he made frequent incredulous inquiries.

Although roads were generally better in the south-eastern quarter of England than in the rest of Britain, the county of Sussex seems to have been an exception. The phrase, 'a Sussex bit of road', meant a bad bit of road. No one has put forward a fully satisfactory explanation of why this should have been so; subsoil of clay or chalk, prevalent throughout much of the county, cannot have been the only cause, nor was it simply that the number of people who had occasion to complain was greater in Sussex, as neighbouring counties like Kent and Surrey, just as heavily travelled, never provoked quite such a chorus of disgruntlement. According to some figures published in *The Times* in 1825 (quoted by John Copeland), £149 per mile was spent annualy on repair of roads in Surrey, whereas the figure for Sussex was only £70; however, a number of other counties spent far less.

The administration of road maintenance in Sussex seems to have been more than usually complicated. A writer who attempted to describe local responsibilities for repairing bridges in the county in 1835 found the task almost beyond him: "The bridges in this county are repaired and maintained in various ways: those called county bridges are repaired as follows:- in the eastern division, out of the general county rates, raised within the same for county purposes; in the western, by rates made on the several Rapes within which the bridges are situate. There are other bridges (not being county bridges) repaired by the Hundreds, Parishes, Tythings or Hamlets, or by certain lands or individuals, but as the custom varies so much, it is almost impossible to ascertain the same with any degree of certainty."

Postlethwayt, in his *Universal Dictionary of Trade and Commerce*, wrote, "I have seen in that horrible country [Sussex], the road 60 to 100 yards broad, lie from side to side all poached with cattle, the land of no manner of benefit and yet no going with a horse, but at every step up to the shoulders, full of sloughs and holes, and covered with standing water". Horace Walpole in the same period remarked that the roads of Sussex were notorious – "Never go to Sussex if you love good roads . . ." – and at about the same time the main street of Petworth was described as "full of deep holes, and a precipice on one side of the street, without so much as a rail for twenty yards". Fifty years earlier, the situation in the town might have seemed less shocking because of the extreme difficulty of getting there in the first place. Prince George of Denmark travelled to Petworth by coach from Windsor in 1702. The journey took fourteen hours and although, we are told, the coach was only overturned once, it "would have suffered much if the nimble boors of Sussex had not frequently poised it or supported it with their shoulders from Godalming almost to Petworth . . . The last nine miles of the way cost us about six hours to conquer them; and indeed we had never done it if our good master had not, several times, lent us a pair of horses . . . whereby we were able to trace out a road for him". Except in a few places, winter travel was impossible for any wheeled vehicles in Sussex at the end of the eighteenth century. A doctor, eyeing the local talent as he made slow and sticky progress on his rounds, pondered on the long legs of Sussex girls and concluded that they were developed by the exercise of constantly pulling their feet out of the mud.

From the groans that resound from the pages of almost every traveller in Britain between the sixteenth century and the nineteenth, it is obvious that road conditions really were bad, and at first sight it would appear that they were continually getting worse. In fact, that impression is probably false. Increasing complaint is to be explained by increasing travel rather than deteriorating roads, and although none of the measures undertaken by governments and local authorities to improve matters came anywhere near achieving the results desired, nevertheless there was probably a slight overall improvement in the roads in the hundred years before 1750.

THREE

Horse, Wagon And Shank's Mare

Confronted with "cledgie soiles", "miry ways" and "hugeous stones", people preferred to travel on horseback. Queen Elizabeth herself often rode pillion, holding on to the broad leather belt of the rider (it would be interesting to know what dress she wore – not her usual immense skirts, presumably). She rode thus from Ipswich to Norwich in 1578, while her ladies jolted along in coaches. On more stately occasions, the Queen felt that a coach was necessary, but it was a mode of conveyance she did not like. She complained of aches and pains the day after a coach journey.

For others, riding was expensive. The quickest way was to hire a horse (and usually a guide too) in each town, this service being provided by postmasters, who were also innkeepers. A man travelling from London to Plymouth by this means in about 1600 would have paid, altogether, something approaching £5. 'Posting' was therefore relatively more costly than air travel today. It was also, by modern standards, far from quick; five miles an hour was an exceptionally good average speed in most parts of Britain. Some people believed that to send a message a longish distance, a 'footpost' was quicker. The best messengers were Irishmen; they cultivated thick ankles and wore their hair in a bush flopping over the forehead – said to be useful for concealing secret messages. Lord Berkeley's footman once covered 148 miles to fetch medicine for his master's lady in forty-two hours, which included a night's sleep.

The fastest method of travelling was to persuade the relevant court official to entrust you with the government mail. This bestowed the right to commandeer horses at any place in the king's name, and to pay for them at the official government rate which, needless to say, was lower than the rate charged to ordinary travellers. Few people were in a position to obtain perquisites of this sort, although riding hard into a town and demanding a new mount in an aggressive manner while waving an official-looking document could sometimes work wonders. Enough bluffs of this kind were pulled off to provoke government action against "People of evil Condition which, of their own Authority take and cause to be taken royally Horses and other things".

Riding was expensive in other ways too, particularly in wear and tear on clothes. A pair of riding boots began to deteriorate after a few longish journeys. One hard-riding courtier is said to have regularly purchased two new pairs during the course of a journey. In addition, the wise traveller was well-cloaked with a garment that came down below the tops of his boots, and well-armed against attack by highwaymen.

Another drawback to hiring horses was the questionable quality of the beasts provided. No sensible man would entrust a valuable horse to the average traveller, whose only interest was in reaching the next town as quickly as possible. The nags supplied by the Cambridge carrier, Hobson, in the early seventeenth century were notorious, though as Hobson's clients were mainly undergraduates, his horses were perhaps more likely to be driven hard than most. He kept a stable of forty, but customers were not allowed to choose, they had to take the first horse offered (the origin of 'Hobson's choice'). Hobson's horses were in frequent use, as the attitude of the dons towards students keeping private horses was much the same as it is now (or was not long ago) towards students keeping private cars. The water poet John Taylor has a nice example of undergraduate wit in connection with Hobson's hacks. "Twelve scholars riding together, one of them said 'My Masters, let us ride faster.' 'Why?' quoth another, 'methinks we ride a good pace; I'll warrant it is four miles an hour.' 'Alas!' said the first, 'What is four miles an hour amongst all of us?'"

On the London-Dover road, there seems to have been an efficient posting system in operation before the end of the fourteenth century. This was probably the most travelled road in

England, at least by men of substance, as it was the chief link with the continent. The traffic was anyway sufficient for a group of men to set up staging posts for hired horses. The horses were trained to perform a "false gallop after some ten miles an hour". Such a pace became known as a 'Canterbury gallop', subsequently shortened to 'canter'.

During the sixteenth century the Dover road system became part of the nation-wide royal post, in which the 'packet' was carried from town to town by 'postboys' (many of them quite elderly) carrying their despatch bag and blowing their horn every quarter-mile to prove that they were active in the king's business and not asleep under a shady tree.

Those who could not afford to ride – the vast majority of the population – used their feet, if they travelled at all. We have forgotten rather quickly how far our ancestors were accustomed to walk. Nowadays few people would contemplate making a journey of more than a mile or so on foot, but a hundred years ago ordinary people thought nothing of walking fifteen or twenty miles and arriving in time for lunch – unless it should be that country-living authors of numerous Victorian memoirs happened to be unusually vigorous in this respect. In earlier times, when an average speed of five miles an hour was a good rate by the fastest means of travel available, walking did not seem so inconvenient a way of getting about.

There was a third method of travel – by the carrier's wagon. By the end of the sixteenth century most towns of any size had at least one professional carrier, generally a citizen of some standing, whose 'long wagon' might hold as many as twenty people. This passenger traffic was said by Stow to have begun about 1564, but it was never very popular. Though cheaper than hiring horses, it was expensive. It was also uncomfortable and extremely slow. When Roderick Random and his friend Strap, growing footsore on their walk to London, inquired at an inn if there were cheap transport available, they were told "that the wagon from Newcastle to London had halted there two nights ago; and that it would be an easy matter to overtake it, if not the next day, at farthest the day after next". The wagon was used only by those who had no alternative. "This kind of journeying is very tedious", Fynes Morison reported in 1617, "so that none but women and people of inferior condition travel in this sort".

Travel in any kind of vehicle was regarded as degenerate: "in Sir Philip Sidney's time", said John Aubrey, "'twas as much a disgrace for a cavalier to be seen in London riding in a coach in the street as now 'twould be to be seen in a petticoate", and this prejudice persisted into the eighteenth century. But the carrier's wagon bore a definite social stigma. To say of a country girl in London that she had 'come up with the carrier' was to imply that she was no better than she ought to be. The young woman in the Newcastle wagon, when Roderick Random and Strap caught up with it, turned out to be a courtesan. Little Nell, who incidentally found the wagon "a soothing, luxurious, drowsy way of travelling", was, needless to say, an exception.

The carrier, a familiar figure on the road long before the age of stage-coaches, also outlasted them. The horse-drawn wagon or van remained a familiar sight, especially in country districts, well into the twentieth century. He has not entirely vanished even now, and the brewers who still employ horses to supply their pubs with beer claim that there are sound economic reasons for doing so as well as good advertising.

Besides the dangerous condition of the roads, there were other hazards that the traveller had to contend with in the sixteenth and seventeenth centuries, which seldom cause much of a problem today. In a country with about one tenth of its present population, where large stretches of land were wilderness and where signposts were few and far between, a man stranded through some mishap in an inconvenient spot could find himself in serious straits.

Salisbury Plain, though quite heavily travelled, was a notoriously bleak region where disasters were not infrequent. A sudden and fierce storm two days before Christmas in the year 1684 caught many of the local carriers far from shelter and inflicted many casualties. The Shaftesbury carrier was so badly frostbitten that he lost the use of both his hands. The Tunbridge Wells carrier was forced to leave the body of his young son by the roadside after staggering on for miles with the dead child in his arms. A married couple who were riding in company with the Taunton and Tiverton carrier lost contact with the rest of their party and froze to death in a field. A correspondent in Yeovil, writing a day or two later, said that there were still about thirty people missing from his district alone.

Then there was the danger of robbery. Highwaymen, like pirates, have become romantic figures, and it is easy to suppose, from popular stories, that for anyone to complete a journey in England before the nineteenth century without encountering one of these gentlemanly rogues in tricorn hat, frockcoat and mask was unusual. But, obviously, the majority of journeys were concluded in safety. The chances of being robbed on an English highway in, say, the last decades of the seventeenth century were probably not much greater than the chances of being robbed in most American cities today.

Still, it was a problem, especially in the period after the Civil War when some men found it difficult to break the habit of violence they had acquired in that conflict. Many of the stories of the 'gentleman-highwayman' date from this period. Undoubtedly there were such men, but the typical highwayman was not a romantic figure of flashing silver and flowing velvet mounted on a splendid steed, but a rough lout, like the worst of Falstaff's hangers-on, wielding a club or a knife. There may have been ladies glad to hand over their purse to a tall masked figure who spoke as though he were a gentleman driven by ill fortune or evil plots to make his living on the highway, like the oddly named 'Nut Brown Roger' in the once-popular children's story; but John Evelyn's account of his encounter with highwaymen in Kent seems more typical.

> The weather being hot, and having sent my man on before, I rode negligently under favour of the shade, till, within three miles of Bromley . . . two cut-throats started out, and striking with long staves at the horse, and taking hold of the reins, threw me down, took my sword, and hauled me into a deep thicket some quarter of a mile from the highway, where they might surely rob me, as they soon did. What they got of money was not considerable, but they took two rings, the one an emerald with diamonds, the other an onyx, and a pair of buckles set with rubies and diamonds, which were of value, and after all bound my hands behind me, and my feet, having before pulled off my boots; they then set me against an oak, with most bloody threats to cut my throat if I offered to cry out, or make any noise, for they should be within hearing, I not being the person they looked for. I told them that if they had not basely surprised me they would not have had so easy a prize, and that it would teach me never to ride under a hedge . . .

In accordance with the advice of a reformed highwayman turned writer, carriers usually travelled together – but spaced out in a long line, not bunched, so that it was impossible for a band of thieves to surround them. All the wagons heading for one part of the country would set out from London on the same day for mutual protection. Individual riders often accompanied the carriers for the same reason. Some carriers on particularly vulnerable routes apparently paid 'protection money' to highwaymen in the late seventeenth century to ensure themselves against robbery (more orthodox insurance was not available), and there were a few cases, suspected if not always proved, of carriers and highwaymen acting in collusion, just as there were some dishonest innkeepers who passed information about their guests to undesirable acquaintances farther along the road. Wise passengers checked that their pistols were still charged after leaving an inn.

William Blew relates the story of a lad who unwisely boasted at the inn where he stopped for dinner that he had just sold his father's cow for the good price of eight guineas. Resuming his journey, he was soon stopped by a mounted highwayman who requested him to hand over precisely that sum. Fortunately, the lad had more wits than his dangerous chattiness suggested. He contrived to spill the money on the ground, and while the highwayman was picking it up leapt on to the robber's horse and galloped off. The horse was reckoned to be worthy twenty guineas and a further sixteen were later found sewn into the saddle. Most encounters with the 'gentlemen of the road' ended less happily for the innocent traveller.

FOUR

Upstart Coaches

The increase in wheeled traffic generally towards the end of the
sixteenth century was criticized on various grounds. People of
more than normally conservative inclinations tend to be
disturbed more violently by advances in the field of transport
than almost any other – and with good reason, for there are few
greater agents for change. Many of the warnings uttered against
the coach sprang from the same kind of misgivings that prompted
later outcries against the railway, the motor car and the
supersonic airliner. Some of the economic arguments advanced
against the coach now sound curious, to say the least, but there
were also minority groups who saw their livelihood menaced by
the rumbling monsters.

According to a pamphlet published in 1636 and entitled *Coach
and Sedan Pleasantly Disputing for Place and Precedence*, there were
then about 6,000 carriages in London and the suburbs, most of
them private but including several hundred hackney cabs. At that
time there were several thousand watermen on the Thames who
had previously enjoyed a monopoly of public transport. They
fiercely resented the new competitors: "The sculler told him that
he was now out of cash, it was a hard time; he doubts there is
some secret bridge made over to hell, and that they steal thither
in coaches . . . ."* The boatman who comments on the dispute in
Coach and Sedan thinks that "they deserve both to be thrown into
the Thames, and but for stopping the channel I would they were,
for I am sure when I was wont to have eight or ten fares in a
morning, I now scarce get two in a whole day".

*Thomas Decker, 1607

The boatmen had a remarkable spokesman in the person of the attractive 'water poet', John Taylor, whose *The World Runnes on Wheeles* (written in prose, the author informs us, because he was lame at the time and anyway could not think of any words to rhyme with coach except "broach, Roach and encroach") attacked the coach as "a close hypocrite, for it hath a cover for any knavery and curtains to veil or shadow any wickedness". (The government was also troubled by the idea that people could travel about unseen, though its fears were political rather than moral.) Sir Philip Sidney, Sir Francis Drake and Sir John Norris, says Taylor, never rode in coaches because those gallants "were deadly foes to all sloth and effeminacy", though he has to admit that there was another reason – "there were but few Coaches in most of their times".

The rhyming problem notwithstanding, Taylor renewed his attack in verse. He remembered a time,

> [When] upstart Helcart-Coaches were to seeke,
> A man could scarce see twenty in a weeke,
> But now I thinke a man may daily see,
> More than the Wherries on the Thames can be.
> When Queen Elizabeth came to the Crowne,
> A Coach in England then was scarcely knowne,
> Then 'twas as rare to see one, as to spy
> A Tradesman that had never told a lye.

A more heated attack was made in a work with the reassuring title *The Grand Concern of England Explained* . . . by John Cresset, published in 1663. Coaches have become "one of the greatest mischiefs that have happened of late years to the kingdom – mischievous to the public, destructive to trade, and prejudicial to lands". An over-indulgence in the decadent habit of coaching has dire effects on the morale of individuals: "They become weary and listless when they ride a few miles, unwilling to get on horseback, and unable to endure frost, snow or rain, or to lodge in the fields". In short the country was, as usual, going to the dogs.

The author, though still exaggerating, is more convincing when he talks about the damage done to provincial crafts. Country tailors once did good business with the gentry, but communications with London enabled their richer customers to transfer their orders to more fashionable establishments in the metropolis. Local crafts no doubt did suffer in such ways but, it hardly needs to be said, the essential prerequisites for economic advance were better communications and transport. Whatever the ultimate importance of the railways, the Industrial Revolution in Britain – or, at least, its decisive first stage – took place before the railways were built. Nature's generosity in the matter of navigable rivers, and the enterprise of canal-builders like the Duke of Bridgewater, were certainly important, but efficiency in road transport was no less so.

Allowing for some exaggeration on the part of the opponents of the coach, it is still clear that wheeled carriages were a common sight in London by about 1600. The majority of them were privately owned, but there were plenty also for hire – at a cost of ten shillings a day including two horses. Coachmen were already acquiring a reputation as a rough and disrespectful lot, who were willing to solve any dispute over the fare with their fists. Hackney carriages had usually seen better days in private ownership, as the appearance on their sides of decaying coats of arms revealed.

The first coaches were probably imported from central Europe, often via the Low Countries where they were more common than in England, but the fittings and decoration were added in London. As their owners were fairly wealthy people, the fittings were luxurious, and often cost as much as the vehicle itself. The coachmaker's trade soon became a profitable one, and in 1619, was described as "the most gainefullest about the towne".

Though initial outlay was large, a coach could prove a money-saver. A lady paying a visit in the country was formerly accompanied by half a dozen attendants, carrying her various accoutrements and upholding, by their numbers, her social status. But the same lady could travel in a coach with one gentlewoman in charge of all her shawls, cloaks, workbaskets and whatnot without losing face. As Professor Croft suggests, the coach provided a slight but definite impulse towards egalitarianism, evidence of which is provided by the attempts of the Establishment to restrict the use of coaches by legislation and by the absurdities of etiquette, worthy of Versailles, which soon grew up around the coach. For instance, only the coachman of a countess was supposed to drive bare-headed; thus, if the hat of some lesser person's coachman happened to blow off, she would forbid him to stop to retrieve it and spend the rest of the journey hugging herself with satisfaction at the impression being made on passers-by. In Germany, the number of horses drawing the coach was regulated by the rank of the occupant.

It is perhaps to these early days of the private carriage that the origins of that pleasant institution, the picnic, can be traced. It became a simple matter to drive out of town to some attractive spot in the neighbourhood of Croydon or Uxbridge, spend a few hours in pastoral contentment and drive back well before dark. This custom no doubt accounts for the improved condition of the roads in the immediate vicinity of London, along with the needs of persons compelled to dwell outside the city, like the headmaster of Harrow who rebuilt the Harrow road. However, except within a radius of twenty-five or thirty miles from the capital, and on the Dover road, even private carriages were a rare sight before the Civil War.

It is impossible to be sure what the early coaches looked like, or whether they were properly coaches at all. Certainly there were coaches with some kind of suspension in Germany and the Low Countries about 1550 and in France and England soon after. They were slow, heavy and rather clumsy vehicles, with leather flaps over the windows and a projecting 'boot' at each side in which an extra passenger, facing outwards, could be accommodated. In this position there was no shelter from rain, and it must have been exceedingly uncomfortable, as a much-quoted letter of 1663 suggests: "I got to London on Saturday last; my journey was noe ways pleasant, being forced to ride in the boote all the way [from Preston]. The company that came up with me were persons of greate qualitie, as Knightes and ladyes. My journey's expense was 30 shillings. This travell hath soe indisposed mee, that I am resolved never to ride up againe in the coatche. I am extremely hott and feverish. What this may tend to I know not. I have not as yet advised my doctor".

In 1579 the Earl of Arundel imported a coach from Germany which caused a great stir. It presumably represented an advance on vehicles then known in England, but in what way it is impossible to say. About 1600, most private coaches were drawn by a pair of horses, though four were becoming more common. The first man to harness six horses to his coach was apparently the Duke of Buckingham. His action was widely regarded as yet another example of that pampered young man's ostentation, and one of his enemies promptly hitched up eight. However, as coaches ventured further afield, six horses became normal (the stage wagons, after all, commonly had eight).

Numerous improvements were introduced in coachmaking during the seventeenth century. A general refinement of line and lightening of construction brought the coach nearer to the vehicle made familiar by the prints of James Pollard and others, though English carriages in general remained heavier in appearance than contemporary models on the continent. German designs seem to have been considered the best, and the 'berlin' (a name applied to different types of carriage in different times) dates from this period. Some private carriages were equipped with hoods, and glazed windows first appeared on the Duke of York's coach in 1661. Various attempts were made to install steel springs; Pepys inspected one such effort in 1665 and pronounced it "very fine". But they did not catch on, presumably because they were inefficient. Leather braces remained the rule.

Coaches for ceremonial purposes were exceedingly grand. They carried diplomatic weight: an important foreign visitor would expect to be conveyed through London in the King's coach, not the Lord Mayor's or any humbler vehicle, just as today he would expect a Rolls Royce and not a Ford. Such coaches were masterpieces of baroque design. Ralph Strauss quotes a description of a silver coach built for an important marriage in the Farnese family in 1629. The body

was lined with crimson velvet and gold thread, and the woodwork covered with silver plates, chased and embossed and perforated, in low relief . . . The roof was supported by eight silver columns, on the roof were eight silver vases, and unicorns' heads and lilies in high relief projected from the roof and ends of the body here and there. The roof was composed of twenty sticks, converging from the edge to the centre, which was crowned with a great rose, with silver leaves on the outside, and inside by the armorial bearings of the Princes of Tuscany and Farnese held up by cupids. The curtains of the side and back of the coach were of crimson velvet, embroidered with silver lilies with gold leaves. At the back and front . . . were statues of unicorns, surrounded by cupids and wreathed with lilies, grouped round the standards, from which the body was suspended; on the tops of the standards were silver vases, with festoons of fruit, and wrought in silver. In front were also statues of Justice and Mercy, supporting the coachman's seat . . . It is said that twentyfive excellent silversmiths worked at this coach for two years, and used up 1600 lbs of silver.

Private citizens could seldom rise to such heights of flamboyance, but they were ready to spend every penny they could afford, and sometimes more, on their own carriage. With what loving care did Samuel Pepys order and plan his own coach, which eventually arrived "to my great content, it being mighty pretty". With what satisfaction did he set out into the town. "Abroad with my wife, the first time that ever I rode in my own coach, which do make my heart rejoice, and praise God . . .".

The first regular stage-coach, as distinct from hired coaches or carriers' wagons, probably appeared in the 1630s. By 1640 there were several arriving in London each week, though with one exception (Cambridge) their points of departure were all within thirty miles of the capital. They were large, low-slung vehicles holding six or eight passengers. The windows remained unglazed until 1680, the roofs were convex, and the heavy wooden body was slung on thick leather straps running between posts emerging from the axle-trees, which sufficiently reduced the jolting so that the horses could proceed at a trot rather than – as with wagons – a walk. As the coach moved along it swung from side to side like a pendulum, building up a momentum that had a bad effect on weak stomachs. While swinging easily from side to side and moving slightly up and down, it had very little freedom to rock back and forth, placing a considerable strain on the vertical posts. The wheels were – and always remained – the most vulnerable parts, but another common cause of accidents was the snapping of these upright supports. Travel in such a vehicle must have been an ordeal more often than a pleasure, especially in bad weather (though the early stage-coaches did not operate in winter).

Contemporaries, except those inveterately opposed to the whole idea, took a more generous view. "There is of late", said Edward Chamberlayne in the reign of Charles II, "such an admirable commodiousness both for men and women, to travel from London to the principal towns in the country, that the like hath not been known in the world; and that is by stage-coaches, wherein one may be transported to any place sheltered from foul weather and foul ways, free from endangering of one's health and one's body by hard jogging or over-violent motion on horseback; and this not only at the low price of about a shilling for every five miles, but with such velocity and speed in an hour as the foreign post can make but in one day." To folk who had never seen any vehicle more impressive than a farm cart, the first stage-coaches were a marvel, something so extraordinary they could hardly grasp their significance, a sight as strange and wonderful as the first steam trains were to their descendants. Even in Essex, a county bordering on sophisticated London, people were astounded by the appearance of the stage-coach, according to an account drawing on some unidentified source, printed in the *Essex Standard* in 1831 (and quoted by John Copeland). "A coach was a strange monster in those days, and the sight of it put both horses and men into amazement; some said it was a great crab-shell, brought out of China; and some imagined it to be one of the Pagan temples in which the cannibals adored the devil." As late as the 1760s, the appearance of the Danish consul at Falmouth in a coach caused astonishment to the fishermen's families, who called out to each other, "Come and see the house on wheels".

The Civil War interrupted the development of the stage-coach, and it was not until the late 1650s that services began to expand. In the spring of 1658, advertisements appeared for stage-coaches to Exeter and York from the George Inn, Aldersgate. "On Mondays, Wednesdays and Fridays to Salisbury in two days for 20s, Blandford and Dorchester in two days and a half for 30s, Burput [Bridport] in three days for 30s, and Exmaster [Axminster], Hunnington [Honiton] and Exeter in four days for 40s." On the Great North Road, Newark took two and a half days for 30s and York four days for 40s. There was also a coach twice a week to Plymouth (50s) and once a fortnight to Edinburgh (£4). By 1688, stage-coaches were running to London from 88 different towns; by 1705, 180 towns had a London coach service of some kind.

Service was infrequent and slow, and many large towns were not connected with London, or anywhere else. For about one hundred years after its first appearance, the stage-coach remained a comparative rarity. The enthusiastic promises of the early proprietors were not fulfilled. The Chester coach, one of the earliest long-distance stage-coaches, was originally scheduled (before 1660) to complete the journey from London in four days. It is extremely unlikely that it ever maintained this hopeful schedule, for it was taking considerably longer in 1739, according to an account of a journey in that year quoted by Lord William Pitt Lennox:

> In March I changed my Welsh school for one nearer to the capital, and travelled in the Chester stage, then no despicable vehicle for country gentlemen. The first day, with much labour, we got from Chester to Whitchurch, twenty miles; the second day to the 'Welsh Harp', the third to Coventry, the fourth to Northampton, the fifth to Dunstable; and, as a wondrous effort, on the last to London before the commencement of the night. The strain and labour of six horses, sometimes eight, drew us through the slough . . . . We were constantly out two hours before day, and as late at night . . . .

The Exeter coach, according to the advertisement of the George Inn, Aldersgate, in 1658, reached its terminus in four days, but in 1701 it was barely reaching Axminster on the fifth day. Most of the early schedules proved much too optimistic, for which the condition of the roads, along with lazy coachmen, accidents and perhaps disappointing public response, were chiefly to blame. Increasingly there appeared in the advertized schedules of stage-coaches, under the firm announcement of arrival times, a telling parenthetical phrase − "if God permits". Only too often, God did not.

FIVE

Turnpike and Toll

In spite of all difficulties, wheeled traffic increased both in quantity and efficiency throughout the eighteenth century. This could not have happened without improvements in the construction of coaches and carriages and in the administration of stage-coach companies, but better vehicles and better management cannot entirely account for the growing traffic. Clearly, the roads themselves must have improved.

The most serious drawback to the system of parish maintenance of highways was that the people responsible for the improvement and upkeep of the roads were not primarily the people who used them. The inhabitants of a small village in Yorkshire, for instance, had little interest in maintaining several miles of the road from London to Edinburgh which happened to pass through their parish. It was galling to spend valuable time and money on maintaining the highway so that disagreeable strangers could rattle through with greater speed and comfort.

In the Middle Ages there were certain places, mainly bridges, where the traveller was compelled to pay a toll before he could pass. By the seventeenth century tolls had all but disappeared, but the idea that the roads ought to be paid for by those who used them lived on. "Every person ought to contribute to the repair of the roads in proportion to the use they make of, or the convenience they derive from them", said the author of *A Proposal for the Highways* in 1692. By that time tolls had already reappeared in a few places. In fact, a bill to establish tolls on part of what became known as the Great North Road had been put forward nearly sixty years earlier, although it did not go into effect until after the Restoration.

A number of acts were passed in the late seventeenth century empowering the justices of the peace in various districts to erect barriers and levy tolls, but for reasons that are not entirely clear this system was discarded about 1700 and from then on these powers were usually vested in independent local authorities known as Turnpike Trusts. A turnpike was originally the rounded pole, or 'turned pike', that prevented cattle from straying (there are two explanations for the word – one being that the pole was turned in the cabinetmaker's sense and the other that the pole was physically turned like a gate). The term was applied to toll gates and was soon extended to the road itself.

As all the trusts required separate statutes to set them up, they were governed by different regulations; the rates that might be charged and the exemptions that might be made were laid down in each individual act. The members of the trust were local dignitaries, often including the justices, who undertook to build or improve a certain stretch of road in exchange for the right to exact a toll from those who used it. The system of parish labour was not ended, merely transfered to the trust, but as time went by it was increasingly commuted to a cash payment. Statutory labour on the highways, though a nuisance, had never been as harsh a system as the *corvée* in France – one reason, no doubt, why Britain escaped violent revolution on the scale of events in France in 1789. The Surveyor of Highways was now appointed by the trust, but his duties were much the same as the old parish surveyor. The trusts also employed toll-keepers, or pikemen, to man the toll gates. Trusts were usually set up for twenty-one years; it was assumed that by the end of that period there would be no need for anything more than routine maintenance, which could be organized on the traditional system.

This estimate proved too optimistic. Indeed, the turnpike trusts from the first ran into a number of difficulties that, in some cases, made them useless.

In the first place, the trusts often failed to live up to the financial expectations of the trustees. It took a fair amount of capital to set up a trust. John Copeland has published* some detailed accounts of legal expenditure incurred in obtaining the necessary Act of Parliament. In one case legal costs amounted to £468, not an insignificant sum in the eighteenth century, and this

*Roads and Their Traffic

was a case that was not opposed by hostile local interests, as many were. Once the Act had been passed, a toll house had to be built and, sometimes, land had to be purchased for a new road. Surveyors and toll-keepers had to be hired. Many trusts fell into financial arrears when, after some years of operation, their revenue from tolls hardly balanced the interest paid on the capital they had borrowed. Far from enjoying a surplus revenue that could be devoted to the job for which it was intended, many trusts fell behind in the payment of interest on debts and became bankrupt. The main problem was not simply financial miscalculation but human error, idleness, incompetence and corruption – human nature, a cynic might say.

In spite of the minute regulations of most of the turnpike Acts, the trusts, increasingly as time went by, acquired too great a latitude in local administration. They borrowed or spent money recklessly, and they took to farming out the tolls for a flat fee. Here was a great source of corruption. A class of professional toll farmers grew up, who rented tolls from the trusts all over the country. To prevent malpractice, the government stepped in to insist that if the tolls were farmed out, they had to be auctioned to the highest bidder. The response to this was the growth of a 'ring' like that which was said to exist in the antiques business some years ago, in which auctions were 'fixed' by collusion of the bidders.

A more obvious source of corruption existed at the toll-gates. Although records were supposed to be kept by the toll-keeper, he was often tempted to come to an agreeable 'working relationship' with carriers and others who passed by regularly and were willing to pay a small tip to the pikeman rather than a large toll to the trust. Wagons at many toll-gates were supposed to be weighed, the toll depending on the weight, and great unwieldy cranes were installed for this purpose. Apart from their initial cost, the cranes were difficult to operate, and even an honest toll-keeper must have often preferred to waive this tiresome procedure. In 1812, a correspondent of the *Brighton Herald* complained that the Shoreham Bridge toll-keeper gave no tickets (and thus kept no records), neglected to put up his name as he was bound to do, and refused to give his name when asked. Pikemen, whatever the advantages of their way of life, were noted for unsociability. "They're all on 'em men as has met vith some disappointment in life", according to Tony Weller. "Consequence of vich, they retires from the world, and shuts themselves up in pikes; partly with the view of being solitary, and partly to rewenge themselves on mankind, by takin' tolls."

In many parts of the country the inhabitants devised means of avoiding the toll, and in order to catch those who used a part of the turnpike but circumvented the gate, the trusts were sometimes forced to erect more barriers than would otherwise have been necessary. No less a person than William Pitt, in company with his colleagues Dundas and Thurlow, was not above dodging the toll when he found the gate open, narrowly avoiding a backfull of lead from the blunderbuss of the enraged pikeman, who did not recognise the miscreants. It was late at night, and the three statesmen were described as "elevated above their normal prudence".

The trusts gradually acquired various additions to their powers, with effects that were, on the whole, undesirable. Sometimes they won the right to shut off by-roads in order to force local traffic to use the turnpike. From similar motives they opposed the creation of new turnpikes likely to attract some of the traffic away from their own road. As the trustees were usually local men of means, local rivalries and local influence rather than public convenience or common sense often directed what route the road should take. As with the railways a century later, powerful landlords competed for the advantage of having the highway at their gates. Speaking of a turnpike act for a road in east Dorset, Ronald Good says: "The interesting thing about this Act is how the proposals in it ever came to be made, and indeed were it not that a plan of them exists, it would be hard to comprehend them. . . . The proposed road, had it been built, would merely have duplicated the existing road through Lychett, and how, bearing in mind the cost of the inevitable bridge, it could ever have been expected to pay, is difficult to understand." It seems a reasonable guess that some powerful local influence was at work here, as in thousands more anomalies of the turnpikes.

The new roads were sometimes built on routes unsuitable for wheeled vehicles in order to save money by utilizing old packhorse trails. The apparently pointless meandering of some roads today can be traced back to these times. As McAdam was to point out with some force, the turnpikes did not amount to a national system of roads. They arose almost arbitrarily, and a traveller on any important road might find the surface below his wheels or his horse's hooves changing dramatically every few miles as he arrived and departed from a stretch of turnpike. None of the major highways was turnpike throughout its length until the early nineteenth century.

There were many reasons for dissatisfaction with the turnpikes. Indirect evidence of their failure to solve the roads problem is provided by the mass of legislation on highways enacted during the eighteenth century and collated in the General Turnpike Act of 1733, which was widely acknowledged to be so complicated that no one could be expected to understand it.

Locally, the appearance of a toll-gate on the road provoked intense disgust that often manifested itself in violence. People who had to use the road daily felt their livelihood threatened, and their resentment increased when they saw, as they often did, that the iniquitous tolls failed to bring any improvement to the roads. There were riots at places in the West Country in the 1720s; toll-houses were burned and toll-keepers roughed up. At Bristol in 1749 a mob armed with "rusty swords, pitchforks, axes, guns, pistols, clubs, etc . . . ranged themselves in the main street before the George Inn. . . . Here they drank freely, with much noise, and then broke the windows of one Mr Durbin . . . who had, by order of the Commissioners, carried persons concerned in destroying the turnpikes before two Justices, by whom they were committed to Newgate." Similar disturbances occurred sporadically well into the nineteenth century. The last major outbreak was in Wales in 1843, when the rioters dressed as women and called themselves 'Rebecca's daughters', after the Rebecca in Genesis who is instructed: "Be thou the mother of thousands of millions, and let thy seed possess the gate of those which hate them". This revolt showed signs of developing a broader base before it was suppressed by soldiers and a bevy of London bobbies. A commission of inquiry later ordered the removal of the toll-gates that had started the trouble.

The surveyors appointed by the turnpike trusts, or by the contractors who farmed the tolls, were usually no more knowledgeable than the surveyors appointed by the parish. In Surrey, it was said in 1794, "a knowledge of the fundamental principles of making roads is not deemed at all necessary [and] the Surveyor . . . may be a carpenter, a bricklayer or any other profession . . .". However, the turnpike surveyors had the advantage that they often held office, even if part-time, for longer than their predecessors and thus, if reasonably conscientious and intelligent, acquired knowledge through experience. If they had no awareness of "the fundamental principles of making roads", that was not their fault, for it could hardly be said in eighteenth-century Britain that there were any such principles. A great range of methods for road construction were advocated, some sensible, some very doubtful, like the "angular road sloping like a pantile roof from one hand to the other". By the end of the century some people had become aware of such matters as the importance of good drainage, but even Telford and McAdam were to formulate quite different methods of laying a good road.

Up to about the middle of the century, it was arguable whether the turnpikes had improved the general road system at all. Robert Phillips, in 1737, thought that wrong-headed methods had actually made the situation worse: "[the] turnpike roads, instead of being mended, have been made bad by art. . . . If the turnpikes were taken down, and the roads not touched for seven years, they would be a great deal better than they are now". A report to the Board of Agriculture towards the end of the century stated that "most of the *parish highways* in [Middlesex] are superior to any other of equal extent I have ever seen. . . . The *turnpike roads*, on the contrary, are generally very bad; although at the toll-gates of this county there is collected a very large sum of money, probably not less than £130,000 a year, which is uselessly expended. ..." Reports from a number of other countries, however, uttered favourable verdicts on the turnpikes, and on the whole opponents of the turnpikes in the eighteenth century were outnumbered by their supporters. "There never was a more astonishing revolution accomplished in the internal system of any country", wrote one enthusiast in 1767. "It is probable that there is no one circumstance which will contribute to characterize the present age to posterity so much as the improvements which have been made in our public roads."

However slow and haphazard, major improvement of the chief highways was the eventual result of the turnpike system. After about 1750, turnpike acts multiplied rapidly, which they would hardly have done if they had been unsuccessful. In 1750 there were about 200 turnpike trusts in existence; twenty years later there were over 500. By 1830, in the golden age of coaching, 20,000 miles of public roads (ten per cent of the total) were turnpikes. They certainly fell far short of the desirable goal of providing an adequate national road network. But that was not a practical aim in the eighteenth century. For all its drawbacks, the turnpike system was probably the best available in the context of the time.

SIX

Superior Vehicles

According to the author of *A Treatise on Carriages*, published in 1794, "in the year 1790, the art of Coachbuilding had been in a gradual state of improvement for half a century past, and had now arrived to a very high degree of perfection, with respect both to the beauty, strength, and elegance of our English carriages". A government employee a few years later added, "in the variety of construction of public carriages for the conveyance of passengers London excels all other places". Foreigners were less certain of British superiority. A French writer, commenting in 1770 on the popularity of a carriage similar to the English postchaise, remarked, "it is no doubt sufficient that the invention of this vehicle comes from England to make all the world desire to have them, as if there existed some law which obliges us to be the servile imitators of a nation that is our rival and which, although it is respectable, and admirable even, in some respects, can never be equal to us for works of taste in general, and above all in Coachbuilding". Commenting on this argument a century later, G.A. Thrupp conceded that "although we have the name for superior vehicles, and deservedly so as regards quality, durability, and ease, the French are beyond us in applying tasteful painting, trimming, and decoration of all sorts".

Whether the French would be happy with this division of the laurels seems doubtful. Nevertheless, by the end of the eighteenth century English coachbuilders were widely acknowledged as the best, and vehicles were a small but significant item in Britain's export trade; Edinburgh coachmakers found customers in Russia and the Baltic countries. The increasing efficiency of coaches runs roughly parallel with the improvement of roads, for it was not until the second half of the century that substantial advances were made.

By comparison with the profusion of nineteenth-century coaching prints, information about the appearance of stage-coaches in the first half of the eighteenth century is quite sparse. According to an often-quoted description of later date, they were

> constructed principally of a dull black leather, thickly studded, by way of ornament, with black-headed nails tracing out the panels; in the upper tier of which were four oval windows, with heavy red wooden frames, and green stuff or leathern curtains. Upon the doors . . . there were displayed in large characters the names of the places whence the coach started, and whither it went, stated in quaint and ancient language. The Vehicles themselves varied in shape. . . . The roofs of the coaches, in most cases, rose into a swelling curve, which was sometimes surrounded by a high iron guard. . . . The coachman, and the guard . . . then sat together; not as at present, upon a close, compact varnished seat, but over a very long and narrow boot, which passed under a large spreading hammer cloth, hanging down on all sides, and finished with a flowing and most luxurious fringe. Behind the coach was the immense basket stretching far and wide beyond the body, to which it was attached by long iron bars or supports passing beneath it. . . . The wheels of these old carriages were large, massive, ill-formed, and usually of a red colour; and the three horses that were affixed to the whole machine – the foremost of which was helped onward by carrying a huge long-legged elf of a postillion, dressed in a cocked hat, with a large green and gold riding coat – were all so far parted from it by the great length of their traces that it was with no little difficulty that the poor animals dragged their unwieldy burthen along the road. It groaned, and creaked, and lumbered, at every fresh tug which they gave it, as a ship, rocking or beating up, through a heavy sea, strains all her timbers with a low-moaning sound, as she drives over the contending waves.

Other evidence emphasizes the importance of the qualifying statement that the vehicles "varied in shape". They varied in other aspects too: four horses, not three, were the usual number; guards were not universally provided; postillions were not always so smart. But any summary of the evolution of the stage-coach in the eighteenth century is bound to suggest a too logical and orderly development. From the evidence of contemporary

1. A postboy, from a drawing by Hugh Thomson, about 1890.

2. A packhorse, from an early nineteenth-century print. Coal was still transported in the baskets of packhorses in many parts of England in the eighteenth century.

3. "The Kendal Flying Waggon", by Rowlandson, 1816. "Flying" was something of a misnomer as the old stage-wagon travelled at less than walking pace. Nevertheless, it had a long life until rendered obsolete by railways, while the local carrier remained a familiar figure in English villages up to the First World War.

4. A coach in the time of Charles II, when they were still widely regarded as a form of conveyance fit only for women.

5. The ceremonial coach of the Portuguese ambassador to the Vatican in the eighteenth century, when rococo decoration almost obscured the function of the vehicle.

YORK Four Days Stage-Coach.

Begins on Friday the 12th of April 1706.

ALL that are defirous to pafs from *London* to *York*, or from *York* to *London*, or any other Place on that Road; Let them Repair to the *Black Swan* in *Holbourn* in *London*, and to the *Black Swan* in *Coney-ftreet* in *York.*

At both which Places, they may be received in a Stage Coach every *Monday, Wednefday* and *Friday,* which performs the whole Journey in Four Days, (*if God permits.*) And fets forth at *Five* in the Morning.

And returns from *York* to *Stamford* in two days, and from *Stamford* by *Huntington* to *London* in two days more. And the like Stages on their return.

Allowing each Paffenger 14l, weight, and all above 3d. a Pound.

Performed By { Benjamin Kingman, Henry Harrifon, Walter Baynes,

Alfo this gives Notice that Newcaftle Stage Coach, fets out from *York,* every *Monday,* and *Friday,* and from *Newcaftle* every *Monday,* and *Friday.*

[handwritten] red in pt. 05-00. 0 of Mr. Bodingfold for 5 pld or Monday the 3 of June 1706

6. An advertisement for a York–London stage-coach in 1706. Such optimistic schedules were seldom maintained.

hn *Cottington alias Mull Sack Robbing y̆ Oxford Wa*
Wherein he found Four Thousand Pounds in Money

7. A carrier robbed by a highwayman. The popular figure of legend,
well-dressed, well-horsed and armed with silver-mounted pistols, was
a comparative rarity. More common was the roadside thug, leaping
from cover to club a solitary rider.

8. A toll-house at a bridge over the Thames on the Cheltenham and Gloucester road west of Exford. Although the gates have been swept away, many old toll-houses, often hexagonal and usually one-storeyed, can still be seen on British roads.

9. The tollgate at Hyde Park Corner in 1798. A stage-wagon, carving a track in the highway, is approaching town and a "diligence", forerunner of the omnibus, is setting out for the suburbs; gossiping milkmaid at left, St George's Hospital at right.

10, 12. (*Left*) a stage-coach in the mid eighteenth century, with some typical incidents of travel evident in the chasing dogs, the roadside beggar and the steep road requiring the efforts of six horses to move the coach. (*Right*) "Scene in a Country Inn Yard" after Hogarth. The usual large lady is being assisted inside; outside passengers have an uncomfortable station in the basket or a precarious one on the rounded and unguarded roof.

11, 13. (*Above*) John Palmer, from an etching by Martha Jervis and (*right*) the first mail-coach—no different from other light coaches of the type often known as "post" coaches, and painted yellow rather than the dark red that soon became standard. (The Post Office, incidentally, has recently shown signs of reverting from red to yellow.)

14. A mail-coach passing through a village in the small hours picks up mail bags without making a stop.

15. The mud-spattered York mail changing horses at the Marquis of Granby. The new team is backed in under the direction of the coachman (who does not leave his box), while the old team make their way to the stables, the guard checks the baggage, and a passenger reaches down for a drink.

handbills and paintings it is clear that great differences existed; there was never a time when all the coaches on the road conformed to one contemporary pattern.

Besides its generally heavier build, the stage-coach of the eighteenth century differed in several obvious respects from its descendant of the nineteenth. The box on which the coachman sat was separate from the main body of the coach, as it remained until the beginning of the nineteenth century; fears were expressed that if the driver's seat were made more comfortable he would go to sleep and fall off. Also, the box was usually set too low to permit driving four-in-hand (i.e. four reins in one hand – the driver controlling all four horses individually), hence the presence of a postillion on the nearside leader. The roof was still curved and the iron rail around it was not a common feature. One would therefore suppose that riding on the roof was impossible, but some brave spirits managed it somehow, and eventually the coachmasters realised that by taking passengers outside they could increase their income. Thus the flat roof was introduced, with provision for six passengers (three at the front, three at the rear), plus one next to the driver – a favourite position if the weather was fine. This development did not take place until near the end of the century; one effect of it was to make the stage-coach available to a wider section of the public.

The absence of baggage space was responsible for the huge basket over the rear axle. Passengers as well as parcels were carried in the basket, though Pastor Moritz found it a highly uncomfortable situation (*see* Chapter 11). By the end of the century, the basket had evolved into an open box attached to the body and finally into a built-in boot that roughly matched the coachman's box in front.

The chief technical developments of the eighteenth century were the introduction of steel springs and a general lightening of construction, the latter largely following from the former. Steel springs had come into use for private carriages in Pepys's time, but they were not introduced on stage-coaches until much later. The City of London Lord Mayor's coach, first used in 1757, is hung on leather straps, without springs, and the French writer quoted above still doubted that steel springs were advantageous a dozen years later. The date at which they were first installed on a stage-coach is uncertain, but in 1754 an advertisement in the

Ipswich Journal announced that "a handsome Machine, with steel springs for the ease of passengers . . . began on Monday, the 8th of July 1754 . . . from Chelmsford . . . to the Bull Inn, Leadenhall Street. . .". The tone of this announcement suggests that steel springs, though not so extraordinary as to tempt the writer into a lyrical amplification of their virtues, were sufficiently unusual to merit special mention. An Edinburgh coach with the same refinement was advertised in the same year.

The earliest springs were usually small 'elbow' springs at the four corners of the body, attached to leather straps; they were probably not strong enough to withstand the jolts and bumps of any but the smoothest road. The later cee spring, projecting in rococo curves from either end of the body and again attached by leather straps, was more durable but not very stable; it appears to have been responsible for a new use of the word 'bounder'. In 1804 Obadiah Elliot introduced elliptical springs which rested directly on iron axles and banished the necessity for a strong, heavy perch (the beam linking front and rear axles), resulting in the much lighter, safer and more comfortable vehicles of the nineteenth century. The effect of Elliot's elliptical spring on coachbuilding has been compared (by Professor Bagwell) with the multi-tubular boiler on steam-locomotive design. Besides these basic improvements, a bewildering range of different systems and combinations came to be used: in Ralph Strauss's words, "the whole subject is too complicated for the lay mind to understand". But the proliferation of types and the frequent complaints of breakage suggest that the problem of springs was never completely solved in the age of the stage-coach. Various alternatives for private carriages were still being discussed long after the early railway lines had grown rusty.

Somewhere about the middle of the eighteenth century, public coaching reached the economic take-off point. A number of contributing factors, such as better roads and better coaches, combined to create a situation in which the rate of growth acquired self-generating momentum. A better service meant more business; more business meant more profit; more profit meant capital for investment in still better service. For example, the early stage-coaches were frequently drawn by the same horses from their starting point to their destination, because to provide changes of team *en route* was too expensive for a coachmaster

operating one or two coaches a week. The working life of the
wretched animals was short (probably no more than the three or
four years allowed for the hard-pressed mail-coach horses) and,
more to the point from the traveller's point of view, their
performance was poor. It is surprising that they managed to drag
the heavy coaches of the time, over variable roads, for a hundred
miles or more, even once never mind once a week. Naturally,
they could not be driven fast, and if one went lame it was not
always easy to replace it. When coach services expanded, thanks
to increasing custom, relays of horses became practical, and
average speeds therefore improved.

Another development connected with changing horses was the
introduction of set routes and stricter times. When coaches were
rare and passengers few, it was customary for the coachman to
vary his route in order to pick up or let off passengers by pre-
arrangement. The coach did not always stop the night at the same
place on each journey because its timing was so irregular. But
once a system of stages was set up, with horses waiting at fixed
points along the route, a more orderly arrangement became
necessary, while the greater number of people proceeding from
town to town discouraged unscheduled deviations for the sake of
the odd fare. Something of the same sort has happened with
country buses which, thirty or forty years ago, would frequently
make unofficial stops to let off a passenger at a convenient point
but now, with greater efficiency perhaps, proceed inevitably
from stop to stop, their automatic doors firmly sealed against
infringements of their schedule.

Stage-coach services were often started in the provinces,
especially in the rapidly growing towns of the Midlands and the
North, by businessmen who were anxious for easier
communication with the capital. The Birmingham–London
service was begun in 1731 by Nicholas Rothwell of Warwick,
whose coach bill still exists. It promised that his coach would "set
out from the *Swann Inn* in *Birmingham*, every *Monday* at six a
Clock in the Morning, through *Warwick, Banbury* and *Alesbury*,
to the *Red Lion* in *Aldersgate street, London*, every *Wednesday*
Morning". It departed the Red Lion on Thursday at 5 a.m.,
reaching Birmingham on the Saturday (Sunday travelling was
generally avoided). The fare was 21s each passenger, and the free
baggage allowance fourteen pounds (one penny a pound

overweight). Mr Rothwell also ran a weekly wagon from Birmingham to London (which took twice as long as the coach) and offered carriages and horses for hire to travellers.

New stage-coach services began to multiply in the 1750s. In Norwich, the regular weekly coach first rumbled out of the yard of the Maid's Head on a Wednesday morning in 1751, arriving in London in two days (three travelling days – coaches usually started very early in the morning). Several important new routes were opened in 1754, when the following announcement appeared in Newcastle: "A coach will set out towards the end of next week for London, or any place on the road. To be performed in nine days, being three days sooner than any other coach that travels on the road: for which purpose eight stout horses are stationed at proper distances". It was without doubt the relay of horses that allowed this 'Flying Coach' to outpace its predecessors. In the same year a new through-coach from Edinburgh to London was announced; the coach that performed this service in the seventeenth century had soon been abandoned and passengers had to change at Newcastle. The new coach had glass windows and steel springs ("exceeding light and easy") and operated once a fortnight throughout the year. The advertised time for the journey was ten days in summer and twelve days in winter; at that time forty miles a day was regarded, theoretically anyway, as a reasonable average. The London-Exeter coach was supposed to take three and a half days but usually took much longer. The Manchester 'Flying Coach', also started in 1754, promised to perform the journey to London in four and a half days, "however incredible it may appear". Stage-coaches from Liverpool and Leeds, begun soon afterwards, had similar schedules.

During the following three decades, stage-coach times were considerably reduced. The Newcastle-London coach reached its destination in less than four days in 1785; the Manchester coach was down to two days by the same date. The 120 miles from Bristol to London which, thanks partly to fashionable patronage of Bath, was one of the best roads in the country, was covered in two days in 1750; by 1780 it was down to eighteen hours. Competition from the mail-coaches after 1784 encouraged still faster times. These dramatic reductions were achieved by better organization of fresh horses and by travelling through the night –

at the cost of antagonizing many innkeepers who saw their old customers passing their door in a cloud of dust where once they had stopped for food and rest.

Unusual events always command greater publicity than the commonplace. The rapid times achieved by some of the stage-coaches, which struck people with amazement or trepidation, were exceptional, and were only possible on three or four of the main roads. Elsewhere, journey times did not improve much in the second half of the eighteenth century. De Quincey recorded that on his first journey (at the age of seven) in 1794, it took nine hours to cover little over forty miles, and added: "This, except on the Bath or great North roads, may be taken as a standard of performance, in 1794 . . . and even ten years later". Yet he was travelling in a postchaise, generally considered faster than a coach.

Most of these coaches carried six passengers inside, and some carried more in the basket or on the roof where they paid half, or a little more than half, the 'inside' fare. The fare from Liverpool to London (197 miles) was two guineas. From Shrewsbury (153 miles) it was one guinea, or half a guinea outside, a comparatively cheap fare probably due to the fact that Shrewsbury had two rival coach companies. Fares began to rise, along with prices generally, in the latter part of the century. Travelling by stage-coach to Scotland in 1800, Thomas Somerville found that the fare had doubled since he had first made the journey, for £7, thirty years earlier.

Provincial cities were also being linked by stage-coaches. At the end of the century coaches left Chester every week for five different destinations – London and Liverpool (two coaches each) Manchester, Shrewsbury and Holyhead. Even Glasgow and Edinburgh, farther apart in spirit than in miles, had their linking stage-coach. In the middle of the century, it was necessary to stop overnight at Falkirk, but by 1770 a coach left Edinburgh every morning except Sunday and reached the Saracen's Head in Glasgow the same night. Coaches also went from Edinburgh to Perth and Stirling, but in spite of the recent road-building in the Highlands, travellers who wished to venture beyond Perth had to adopt other means.

Before the end of the eighteenth century, it was possible to travel to and from most of the cities and large towns in Britain by stage-coach. But the list of services may give a misleading impression of the actual numbers travelling. Six persons leaving Edinburgh for London once a fortnight does not amount to a mass exodus. The steadily accelerating advance of coaching did not hit its peak until the second or third decade of the nineteenth century; in 1800, the number of people who regularly travelled by coach was a minute proportion of the population. For, although coaching was a relatively cheap and (to use a favourite adjective of the proprietors) 'expeditious' method of travel, it was and always remained by absolute standards expensive. It was bound to be. The proprietors' running expenses were large: hire or maintenance of coach and horses; payment of coachman, guard (if any) and stable-hands; turnpike tolls; government duties and taxes. Even if the coach were always full, the proprietor still had to charge what today seem high fares. Competition sometimes brought fares down sharply, but coaching could never become a form of cheap mass transportation. For the majority of the population, it was out of reach.

The diarist Sylas Neville recorded the expenses of his housekeeper's journey from Scratby in Norfolk to Eastbourne in Sussex to fetch her young daughter in the 1770s. From Scratby to Norwich cost three shillings; dinner for herself and the boy accompanying her to Norwich cost 6s 6d. She travelled outside on the coach from Norwich to London for 11s and from London to Lewes for 6s 6d. At Lewes she had to hire a horse and man, for 7s, to reach Eastbourne. On the return journey she again rode outside on the coach from Lewes to London and London to Norwich, with her daughter, who was small enough to sit on her lap, going half-price. This came to 29s. Meals on the road cost 10s. With a few more expenses, the total bill came to over £4, equivalent to something not far short of £100 today. If she had travelled inside the coach, it would have been nearly double.

Still, for those who wished to travel rapidly and in reasonable comfort, the stage-coach was unequalled – unless, of course, they were rich enough to adopt a superior means of travel. The wealthy travelled in their own carriages. On short journeys, a man might drive himself in one of the many types of light carriage which, already visible on the roads in the late eighteenth century, increased both in numbers and variety after the introduction of elliptical springs. The wealthy travelled in their own coaches driven by their own coachman and accompanied by their own servants; if they were in a hurry they hired post horses along the route, if not they used their own horses. Elizabeth Grant of Rothiemurchus recalled her family's annual epic journeys between London and the Highlands about the turn of the century in a

> large *berline* . . . which the four horses must have found heavy enough when weighted with all its imperials, hat boxes, and the great hair trunk. . . . Mrs Lynch and Mackenzie, who had been my father's valet before he married, were on the outside; my father, Jane, and I within with my mother, and we travelled with our own horses ridden by two postillions in green jackets and jockey caps. . . . In the heavy post-chariot behind were the two nurses, the baby in a swinging cot, William, who was too riotous to be near my mother, and a footman in charge of them. What it must have cost to have carried such a party from London to the Highlands! . . . We travelled slowly, thirty miles a day on an average, starting late and stopping early. . . .

Such expeditions were only for the very rich. Apart from the incidental expenses of the journey, the cost of keeping a private coach was estimated (in 1837) at about £200 a year, including coachman's wages.

Posting was probably still the fastest method. The postchaise, or chariot, looked roughly like a coach with the foremost section of the body removed and held two or three passengers. Coaches could also be hired, and people often clubbed together to hire a chaise or a travelling coach. The chaise was drawn by two horses, four when the roads demanded them, and was driven by a postboy riding the nearside horse. It normally travelled at a gallop, while coaches proceeded at a safer – and not much slower – trot. The hire of a chaise and pair cost 9d a mile in the 1760s, rising to 1s and 1s 3d a mile by the end of the century – four or five times as costly as the stage-coach. In *Roads and Their Traffic* John Copeland prints the annual accounts of a Suffolk postmaster in 1802, when he was charging 1s a mile for a chaise and pair and had been accused by the public of profiteering. The acounts showed, in fact, that he was making a slight loss, though a neutral accountant might have arrived at a different conclusion.

SEVEN

Mail On Time

By about 1780 the improved performance of the stage-coach had placed the British Post Office in an anomalous position. The mail was still carried by postboys, or 'mailmen' as they were coming to be called, whose ordained speed of six miles an hour (recently raised from five) failed to match the stage-coach on the chief roads of the country. A letter posted from Bath on a Monday afternoon would not be delivered in London until Wednesday afternoon. If it were sent by the coach, it would arrive on Tuesday morning at about 10 a.m. The result was that many people sent their letters by the coach. But that was illegal. The Post Office had a monopoly of the mails and to send a letter by stage-coach was to defraud the Post Office of its revenue.

There were other reasons for dissatisfaction with the system of mail carrying. The mailmen (or, in a few out-of-the-way places, mailwomen), who had little incentive to perform their duties with despatch, were unreliable. They were sometimes delayed as a result of over-indulgence at a wayside inn, and sometimes intercepted by robbers, for they were unarmed and no match for a determined highwayman. Some of them were themselves not above probing the packets with eager fingers for the crinkle of banknotes. The public was advised to cut the notes in half when sending money by mail and to hold the second batch until notified of the safe arrival of the first.

Although the Post Office officials, like bureaucrats generally, resisted the notion of reform, it was clear that the business of carrying the mail was in need of a major overhaul. In 1782 John Palmer arrived in London with his plans for a completely new system.

Palmer was the son of a prosperous merchant of Bath whose numerous interests included the Theatre Royal, the first theatre in England to receive a royal license outside London. It was with the theatrical side of his father's empire that John Palmer was concerned as a young man, and it was largely the result of his determination and energy that the Theatre Royal in Bath, and a later establishment in Bristol, acquired their licenses.

The young impresario was a businessman first and a lover of the drama a long way second. He was an example of that new breed of energetic, practical men, full of ideas and common sense, who appeared in such astonishing numbers in the late eighteenth and early nineteenth centuries, and he might well have found himself celebrated in the pages of Samuel Smiles. Palmer's impressive if not very attractive qualities are unmistakable in his portraits: the arched brows, strongly aquiline nose and tight mouth suggest a self-assurance bordering on aggressiveness. Here is a man who means to have his own way and will not easily tolerate criticism, well-meant or not.

Nor was it some deep-seated vocation that attracted Palmer to the reform of the mail service. In the words of his biographer, C.R. Clear, "even his ambitions, although guiltless enough, were scarcely of the highest and most altruistic order. He certainly had in view the advancement and improvement of commerce and industry; but this was clearly secondary to his main, but not unnatural objective, to make a considerable fortune as surely and as quickly as possible." His exemplar was Ralph Allen, another citizen of Bath (and said to have been the model for Squire Allworthy in Fielding's *Tom Jones*), who had organized the cross-country postal system in the first half of the century and done rather well out of it. Allen had died in 1764, when Palmer was only about 22 years old, but it is likely that they were acquainted. Palmer frequently cited the large profits made by Allen when complaining of his own miserly – as he thought – treatment.

In Palmer's plan for the reform of the mail, letters would be carried not by solitary postboys but by special coaches running on strict schedules. The operation would be undertaken by the same men, often local postmasters, who ran the stage-coaches, at the rate of 3d per mile (the same cost as a postboy). The additional costs and the profit (if any) of the contractors would be covered by taking parcels (there was no national parcel post

until the days of the railways) and a limited number of passengers
– at first four, inside only. Horses and coachmen would be
provided by the contractor but the guards would be Post Office
employees charged with the safekeeping of the mail and
responsible for ensuring that it reached its destination on time
whatever happened to the coach. Palmer's original suggestion
was that the guards should be soldiers, because such men were
"accustomed to the Discharge of Fire Arms . . . and to the watch
and fatigue of late hours". The mail would be exempt from tolls,
and toll-keepers were to make sure that their gates were open
when they heard the warning blast of the horn as the coach
approached. Postboys had not paid tolls either, but stage-coach
proprietors and others were annoyed that the same exemption
should be enjoyed by mail-coaches, which damaged the roads as
much as other vehicles, and in Scotland this privilege was
withdrawn by an act of 1813.

Palmer's system, he said, would cut delivery times in half, and
such an improvement would justify raising the price of postage.
So confident was he that his scheme would be a success that he
asked for no payment unless it was, in which case he would
receive $2\frac{1}{2}$ per cent of the profits above a stated figure.

Palmer had some useful contacts in London and soon gained
the ear of William Pitt, who was then, at the hoary old age of 23,
Chancellor of the Exchequer. Unfortunately for Palmer, the
government fell before his scheme could be tried, but in
December 1783 Pitt returned to power and, after three months of
tricky manoeuvring, confirmed his ascendancy by winning a
landslide general election.

Although Pitt was keen on Palmer's ideas, others were more
dubious. The Post Office compiled a formidable dossier of
criticisms in three large volumes, partly motivated no doubt by
resentment of outside interference (and on such a scale!) but
containing some reasonable objections also. The experience of
stage-coaches suggested that the strict timing envisaged by
Palmer would be extremely difficult to fulfill. Coaches, unlike
postboys, could not make detours from the main routes, and in
places far from the highway service would deteriorate. Fears
were expressed that the presence of an armed guard would not
prevent robbery but would encourage worse violence. This last
complaint seems dotty, especially as the mails in their early years

proved to be nearly invulnerable to highwaymen; but there was some trouble with guards who were inclined, through boredom or bravado, to blast off their blunderbusses too freely and, in the words of C.G. Harper, "many inoffensive rustics were wounded by guards sportively inclined" (this is perhaps an exaggeration; certainly, there appear to have been no fatalities). However, a great many of the criticisms voiced by the entrenched bureaucrats at the Post Office were either silly or niggling, and there was some justice in Palmer's peppery description of their attitude as "Don't try it at all, lest it should succeed".

The objections were overruled by Pitt who, prompted by Palmer, saw in the increased postage charges an alternative to his unpopular proposal for a tax on coal, and a trial of Palmer's system was arranged for the Bristol and Bath road beginning in August 1784. Five innkeepers along the route agreed to horse the coach at the agreed rate of 3d per mile.

John Palmer was at the Rummer Tavern in Bristol to see the first mail-coach depart at 4 p.m. on 2nd August carrying the London mail and four inside passengers. It left Bath eighty minutes later and arrived at the G.P.O. in London at 9 a.m. the following morning, taking seventeen hours (as Palmer had forecast) and thus halving the old time. It also beat the advertized time of the fastest stage-coach from Bristol by about one hour, its actual time probably by more.

The trial had been ordained for nine days, but there was no question of stopping it at the end of that time. Yet the extension of the scheme to other routes was less speedy than Palmer had hoped. Eight months elapsed before the next mail-coach was introduced, on the London-Norwich road. A few months later, Liverpool and Leeds began mail-coach services and after that a national network was soon established. By 1830, mail-coaches were covering about 12,000 miles of roads in England each night.

Post Office opposition gradually subsided and Palmer's appointment as Surveyor and Comptroller-General of the Post Office gave him full autonomy except that he remained subject to the overall authority of the Postmaster General (the office was usually shared by two men in the eighteenth century though the title remained in the singular). Palmer's relations with them were prickly. The discovery of his clandestine attempts to discredit his superiors' competence eventually led to an open breach and his dismissal from office after nearly eight years. He was given a pension equal to his salary (£3,000 per annum) but had to fight a long, hard battle in Parliament before his 2½ per cent royalty was restored to him (plus a lump sum of £50,000) in 1813, five years before his death.

The early mail-coaches were not specially designed as such. They resembled the fast travelling coaches, called 'post' coaches, of the period, with room for four passengers inside, smaller than most of the stage-coaches on the chief routes. A 'patent' coach designed by John Besant in 1787 became the first model for the standardized mail-coach, and all vehicles were built to this design by Besant's partner, Vidler of Millbank, whose firm continued as sole contractor to the Post Office for forty of the sixty-odd years that mail-coaches were in general use. The coaches were actually owned by Vidler and hired out on a mileage basis. When they had delivered their packets in London each morning, they were immediately driven round to Vidler's sizeable workshops and serviced, returning in time to take the mail out at 8 p.m. the same evening. The various contractors supplied the coachmen and horses; the guard was a Post Office employee.

Besant's 'patent' coach was still a long way from the perfected design of the nineteenth century which is so familiar in Victorian prints. It was awkwardly high – the result of temporary fashion rather than sound technical principles – and the coachman's box was divorced from the body of the coach. At the back, however, the boot was built-in; the great luggage basket seen on stage-coaches of the time had vanished. The guard sat on top of the boot, his feet planted securely on the iron lid of the mail box, his blunderbuss, cutlass and pair of pistols in a handy case, his brass horn to hand and, somewhere about him, a timesheet and a locked chronometer that he could not alter, to be turned over to the postmaster at the end of his stage.

Strict time-keeping was a novel and, as far as the guards were concerned, a tiresome requirement. Whatever their jobs, people still worked roughly according to the sun, for Greenwich Mean Time had not yet been introduced. The notion of 'working to the clock', by no means the least important of the innovations of industrial society, was still foreign to all but a few thousand Lancashire mill-workers. It has been suggested that it was the mail-coach, travelling to every part of the country, that spread throughout Britain the idea that punctuality was important, which by the middle of the nineteenth century had become an article of life.

Among Besant's technical improvements to the coach, the most useful was his method of attaching wheel to axle by a round metal plate that fitted inside a retaining rim. This did not prevent wheels or axles breaking, but it did greatly reduce the risk of wheels coming off, as they frequently did when secured merely by a pin through the end of the axle. The coach was also provided with an automatic braking system for descending hills, which depended on the weight of the coach, tilted forward by the slope, tightening a strap around the wheel hub; but this ingenious device was apparently ineffective in practice. On steep hills it was still necessary for the guard to jump down and lodge an iron 'shoe' under a wheel to jam it.

Outside passengers were accepted on mail-coaches from about 1803, or when the coachman's box became united with the body of the coach. One passenger sat next to the driver, two or three immediately behind; the guard remained in isolation at the back with a free field of fire. Not until the late 1830s were outside passengers allowed at the back of a mail-coach.

The mails ran through the night, as few coaches had done before 1784, and thus the question of lighting became important. The whale-oil coachlamps, reproductions of which so frequently adorn suburban villas today, were hardly adequate to illuminate the road very far ahead, and could be a danger in case of accident. (Gas lamps, which were advocated towards the end of the coaching age and even tried out on one or two local coaches, were still more dangerous, and the gas tanks took up half the luggage space). One or two coaches, having overturned, were burned by the flame from the lamps setting light to the straw provided to keep the passengers' feet warm. However, such accidents were rare; the speed of travel was not fast and there was little traffic on the roads at night. Also (an obvious but seldom-quoted advantage of the horse over the engine) horses have senses, and may avoid, or give warning of, obstacles that the driver has not noticed.

The early mails (a mail-coach was a 'mail', a stage-coach a 'coach') proved rather fragile, and after Vidler had lost his contract in 1836, strict specifications were laid down, including the type of wood to be used for wheels, perch and axletrees and the total weight of the vehicle – eighteen hundredweight (less than the average stage-coach).

By the 1830s, when they reached their highest efficiency, the British mail-coaches represented the most efficient system of land transportation the world had yet seen, and at their first appearance, when their average speed was generally not more than eight miles an hour, they were recognised as a dramatic step forward (or, according to some opinion, a step towards the abyss). Their speed was astonishing. The German historian, B.G. Niebuhr, travelling to Scotland in 1798, complained that "you can only get a very piecemeal view of the country from the windows, and on account of the tremendous speed, you have no object long in view". John Campbell, the future Lord Chancellor, travelling south by mail-coach in the same year, congratulated himself on his temerity and remarked on the "marvellous celerity, taking only three days and two nights for the whole distance". His family had entreated him to break his journey at York for a day, but he had pressed on although "this speed was thought to be highly dangerous to the head, independently of the perils of an overturn, and stories were told of men and women who, having reached London with such celerity, died suddenly of an affection of the brain".

In spite of the delays at the start, Palmer's system was established with a speed indicative of the rising rate of economic change in the late eighteenth century. A commission appointed to investigate various abuses in the Post Office in 1788 concluded that the mail-coaches were working even better than expected. People received an answer to their letters in less than half the time they had been accustomed to wait and, more important, they could feel certain not only that letters would arrive more quickly, but that they would *arrive*. An additional cause for satisfaction was the increased revenue of the Post Office, some of it initially due to the rise in postal charges but (since the rise continued) mainly the result of increased business and greater efficiency.

The mail-coach was a prestige vehicle, faster, more expensive and indisputably more aristocratic than the stage-coach, which was compelled to give way to the mail when they met on the road. The mailcoaches were uniformly decorated, with restrained elegance, in black and maroon with scarlet wheels. The insignia of the four chivalric orders – Garter, Bath, Thistle and St Patrick – appeared on the panels flanking the windows, and the royal arms on the doors. Only the names of their different routes, neatly stencilled in gold, distinguished one from another. By contrast, the stage-coach was slightly but unmistakeably vulgar, sometimes painted in bright yellow, green or blue, and bearing, in the words of that partisan of the mails, Thomas de Quincey, "as much writing and painting on its sprawling flanks as would have puzzled a decipherer from the tombs of Luxor". Stage-coaches had names, like ships, but mail-coaches were discreetly anonymous, though there was at least one exception, the famous *Quicksilver* Devonport Mail.

Although the stage-coaches soon responded to the challenge, the mails were, from the first, markedly more efficient. Those snappy words like 'despatch', 'celerity' and 'expeditious' that must have seemed ironic to some travellers on the old stage-coaches were well suited to the performance of the mails. The emphasis on strict punctuality was taken seriously by coachmen and guards, especially the latter, who were civil servants and superior to the average stage-coach guard. In their top hats and frogged scarlet coats, the guards – and the coachmen too when by their long service on the mails they gained the honour of a similar uniform – were imposing figures. There were cases of indiscipline; one or two spent time in prison as a result of accidents caused by racing or drunkenness, but the general standard of behaviour was much higher than people were accustomed to on the old coaches.

With their strict schedules, which insisted that time lost at one point should be made up during the next stage, the mails were constantly tempted to go too fast for safety. Legislation laid down that the horses must proceed at a trot, not a gallop, but a mail was within the law so long as at least one horse in the team was trotting. This rule gave rise to that curious and valuable beast, the 'parliamentary horse', whose virtue was that it trotted as fast as the other three galloped, thus permitting high speeds within the limits of the law. Mail-coach contractors at horse sales always kept an eye open for a fast-trotting animal.

The higher speed of the mails was not achieved by any revolutionary procedures, but rather by the improvement of existing arrangements. The first necessity was more frequent change of horses. Some of the slower stage-coaches were still completing long journeys with one team of horses in the 1780s; the early mails made frequent changes and were soon down to an average stage of not much more than eight miles. Even then the working life of the horses was only three or four years. More frequent changing meant more frequent stops, but horses could be changed with remarkable speed. As the mail was so punctual, the ostler would have the fresh horses ready and waiting when it arrived, and with the guard sometimes assisting, the change could be made in a minute or two. The Post Office laid down five minutes as the official time for this operation but with luck three or even four minutes might be gained on the time-schedule. To anyone who has inspected the complicated harness and fittings of a four-horse coach five minutes seems quick – and absolutely correct harnessing was vital, not only for safety but for speed also. "Horses well harnessed are half driven", said Nimrod.

The mails soon developed the knack of dropping off and picking up the mail bags with the minimum delay. At sub-post offices along the route, the guard would drop one bag on the ground and pick up the new one as it was held out towards him on a forked stick, while the coach did not slacken speed.

From the documents ferreted from dusty archives in the G.P.O. by Edmund Vale and published in his book *The Mail-Coach Men*, a picture emerges of the tight control, intelligent planning and administrative efficiency of the management of the mail-coaches in the post-Palmer era. Thomas Hasker, Superintendent of the Mail Coaches from 1792 to 1817, had a tiny staff of assistants and a few surveyors stationed at strategic places in the provinces, yet in spite of his small staff and numerous duties, not least his obligation to keep informed and contented the highclass jobbers who enjoyed the office and emoluments of Postmaster-General, he was personally acquainted with nearly every mail guard in the kingdom, with most of the contractors, and with many of the postmasters.

Within a few days in September, 1796, the indefatigable Hasker is found writing to a dozen people on all kinds of subjects that might have been considered too minute for his attention. To Mail Guard Shugden: "Sir: How could it be possible for you to lose 2 hours 15 minutes in tying up a Spring, which has been frequently done . . . on your road in 10 minutes. Have you got a long bar, a rope, and a chain? I am not determined yet whether I shall suspend you for a month or order you up to the Mail Coach Manufactory to learn how to tie up springs. – T.H." To Mr Vidler at Millbank: "Sir: Pray be so good as to give particular orders that the Coach Axletrees are particularly exmained, as several have broken lately, and I am informed that the Axletree of the Exeter coach that broke on Saturday last had been in a suspicious state for some journeys. – T.H." To Mr Chuck, a contractor at Ware: "Sir: There is great complaints of your harness; it is so rotten that it is dangerous to travel with them. Pray be so good as to supply others, for if I have any further complaint I shall directly send you a new set down [for which Mr Chuck would have to pay]. – T.H."

Though numerous, Hasker's missives were to the point. Brevity was a quality he valued almost as much as punctuality.

It is not easy to account in a few words for the status of the mail-coach in English society. Within twenty years of Palmer's first setting out from Bristol, a national institution had been created. Up and down the country, the mails were regarded with admiration, pride and affection, but with none of the sentimentality that crept in as soon as it appeared that, contrary to the expectations of its originators, the mail-coach was going to have a short life. "In sixty years", wrote F.E. Baines, "the mail-coach was born, attained perfection, and, alas, perished". Lasting less than a human lifetime, the mail-coach remained a comparative novelty; people hardly had time to grow bored with it. Yet the kind of emotion it released in so many people was usually reserved for the most venerable institutions; only the monarchy and the navy inspired comparable feelings. Certainly the railways, though they had many enthusiasts, never produced the same effect – perhaps because they were too strange, too big a break with the past. When the mail-coaches were introduced, people had become accustomed to the idea of long-distance coaching; the mails represented improvement without drastic change, the most comfortable kind of reform.

In a famous essay, De Quincey celebrated the excitement and éclat of the mail-coach in the first years of the nineteenth century, when he was an undergraduate at Oxford, and at the same time put his finger on the reason for its mystique. The profound impression that the mail-coaches made upon him, he wrote, was accomplished,

first, through velocity, at that time unprecedented – for they first revealed the glory of motion; secondly, through grand effects for the eye between lamp-light and the darkness upon solitary roads; thirdly, through animal beauty and power so often displayed in the class of horses selected for this mail service; fourthly, through the conscious presence of a central intellect, that, in the midst of vast distances – of storms, of darkness, or danger – overruled all obstacles into one steady co-operation to a national result.

It was important, De Quincey observed, that the mail was the Royal Mail, almost a descendant of the king's herald whose urgent business it was the duty of every subject to assist.

The connection of the mail with the state and the executive government gave to the whole mail establishment an official grandeur which did us service on the roads, and invested us with seasonable terrors. Not the less impressive were those terrors, because their legal limits were imperfectly ascertained. Look at those turnpike gates; with what deferential hurry, with what an obedient start, they fly open at our approach! Look at that long line of carts and carters ahead, audaciously usurping the very crest of the road. Ah! traitors, they do not hear us yet; but, as soon as the dreadful blast of our horn reaches them with proclamation of our approach, see with what frenzy of trepidation they fly to their horses' heads, and depreciate our wrath by the precipitation of their crane-neck quarterings.

Although, as De Quincey says, the precise extent of the priority enjoyed by the mail was nowhere laid down in black and white, their precedence was widely acknowledged and jealously asserted by the mailmen themselves. There is a story of a mail-coach at the beginning of Queen Victoria's reign encountering a troop of soldiers, for whom all other traffic had made way. As the army was indisputably on the queen's business too, a tricky question of precedence would seem to have arisen, but the mail-coach guard had no doubts. "Drive on, Watson", he shouted angrily to the coachman, and officers and men scattered like chaff.

Riding in his favourite seat on the box next to the coachman of the Holyhead mail one day, the young De Quincey was shocked to see the *Tally-Ho*, a famous Birmingham stage-coach, coming up fast behind. "For some time this Birmingham machine ran along by our side – a piece of familiarity that already of itself seemed to me sufficiently Jacobinical". As the Birmingham coach began to draw ahead, De Quincey grew nervous, but the driver of the mail was merely waiting until his rival believed himself the victor before displaying the superiority of the mail. Then, "he slipped our royal horses like cheetahs, or hunting leopards, after the affrighted game". The mail swept effortlessly past and "threw them into the rear with so lengthening an interval between us, as proved in itself the bitterest mockery of their presumption; whilst our guard blew back a shattering blast of triumph, that was really too painfully full of derision".

The mail was not only the fastest means of transport, it was also the fastest means of communication. It is getting increasingly difficult nowadays to comprehend a society without instant means of communication, when an Act passed in London was unknown in Edinburgh for two or three days and unknown in America for two or three months. It was the function of the mails as bearers of news – what De Quincey called their "awful *political* mission" – that impressed him even more than their velocity, their manifestation of power, or the visual delights that they presented to the traveller. It happened that the period in which the mail-coach system was established was full of dramatic events abroad, for it coincided with the French Revolutionary and Napoleonic wars. "The mail-coach it was that distributed over the face of the land, like the opening of apocalyptic vials, the heart-shaking news of Trafalgar, of Salamanca, of Vittoria, of Waterloo", and "the mail-coach, as the national organ for publishing these mighty events . . . became itself a spiritualized and glorified object".

As self-appointed propagandist for the mail-coach, De Quincey expressed a semi-humorous contempt for the stage-coach, but of course stage-coaches as well as mails carried news to the provinces, although the departure time and greater speed of the mails made them usually the first harbingers in the towns along their routes.

A coach bringing news of a great victory was customarily decked with laurels, so that as soon as it came in sight, the people waiting by the road saw that the news was good. De Quincey himself travelled in a mail-coach leaving London in the evening of the day that news arrived of the battle of Talavera (1809), not one of Wellington's most impressive victories but enough for the street outside the G.P.O. to be filled with "horses, men, carriages, all . . . dressed in laurels and flowers, oak-leaves and ribbons". As they passed through the northern suburbs towards Barnet,

heads of every age crowd to the windows – and rolling volleys of sympathising cheers run along us, behind us, and before us. The beggar, rearing himself against the wall, forgets the lameness – real or assumed – thinks not of his whining trade, but stands erect, with bold exulting smiles, as we pass him. . . . Women and children, from garrets alike and cellars, through infinite London, look down or look up with living eyes upon our gay ribbons and our martial laurels; sometimes kiss their hands; sometimes hang out, as signals of affection, pocket-handkerchiefs, aprons, dusters, anything that, by catching the summer breezes, will express an aerial jubilation.

All this, incidentally, for a battle that resulted in 12,000 casualties and no discernible advantage, military or political, to either side.

The news of the passing of the Great Reform Act, twenty-three years later, was broadcast to the nation by the mail-coach. At Truro in Cornwall on 7th June the town was thronged with people at five o'clock in the morning, waiting for the news. The mail, when it arrived, was loudly cheered, and guns were fired to carry the good news farther. But at Falmouth the mail was beaten to it by a fast steamer which had reached the port from London the previous evening – one of the early victories of coal-burning boilers over horses and wheels.

EIGHT

The Roadbuilders

The transformation in the speed of public transport brought about by the mails naturally affected stage-coaches also. The proprietors of stage-coach companies could not afford to sit still and carry on in the same old way while the mails took their customers. The improved design of coaches – lower and better-sprung – extended to stage-coaches as well as mails; in fact, it is said that the new springs introduced about 1804 which supported the body of the coach – four, in the form of a square, over each axle – were first fitted to a stage-coach, the Manchester *Telegraph*. They were sometimes called 'telegraph' springs.

Around 1800, the stage-coaches were suffering from the competition of the mails; one or two were even taken off the road, and some people feared that the mails would put the stage-coaches out of business. But nothing of the sort occurred. On the contrary, stage-coaches multiplied, especially after about 1820. The main reason was simply that the number of travellers increased to a total far beyond that which the mails could absorb. After all, there were only 27 mails (the number varied somewhat) leaving London each night for every part of the kingdom, and the usual number of seats available on each was seven or eight – not a very great capacity.

With the ever-increasing emphasis on speed, stage-coach schedules were tightened up and stops reduced to a minimum; night-running became normal on long routes. In some cases, stage-coach times matched the mails. In spite of the advantages enjoyed by the mails in freedom from tolls and in taking precedence over all other traffic, a few stage-coaches (which did not have to deliver mail bags) outpaced the mails.

The stage-coach had other advantages over the mail. Not everyone wanted to travel at night, but on the mails night-travelling was unavoidable: the down mails were timed to leave London in the evening and the up mails to arrive in the early morning. Getting a decent meal was extremely difficult on the mail, as it seldom stopped long enough at any one place. A still weightier objection for most people was that the mail cost much more than the stage, in many cases nearly double.

William Chaplin, the greatest of the London coach proprietors who was responsible for about half the mails that left London every night, remarked in about 1835 that people often preferred the stage-coach, leaving the mails short of custom.

> The mails unfortunately do not flourish, except in connection with very populous towns. Now, in Manchester and Liverpool, where there is a vast spirit of enterprise, they esteem the style of travelling by the mail, and we get a very good living; but with respect to places of minor importance, we cannot get a sufficient number of gentlemen or active merchants into the mail . . . Some twenty years ago [1815], when . . . there were no day-coaches for distances of about one hundred miles, gentlemen invariably came from Bath and other such places by the mails . . . but now that day-coaches are established everywhere within a hundred and forty miles of London, all those passengers go by the day-coaches . . . and therefore the mails are very materially suffering.

The mail-coach contractors frequently complained to the Post Office that they could not make a profit, and a few of them actually gave up the business on these grounds. An extra subsidy had to be paid to the contractors who horsed the Newmarket and Norwich mail when the exceptionally fast Norwich *Telegraph* appeared on the road.

But these were minor problems, which the advent of the railways would soon make irrelevant. In 1835, the coaching business was at its height, and the changes that had occurred in the lifetime of Chaplin's generation had made travel by coach far faster, safer, and more reliable than their fathers could have imagined. The remarkable performance of many long-distance coaches in the 1830s filled the British people with pride and struck foreign visitors with amazement. These performances were achieved as the result of better coaches, better horses and better coachmen. But as with earlier progress in land transport, the most important improvement, without which the quality of animals and vehicles hardly counted, was in the condition of the roads.

The rapid increase of turnpike trusts in the second half of the eighteenth century had brought many improvements, but they were patchy and unpredictable; many of the trusts had no knowledge of roadbuilding as a craft. British roads were transformed almost at the end of the coaching age by the work of a small handful of men, in particular by those two practical engineers Thomas Telford and J.L. McAdam.

As far as roads were concerned, Telford was not a great innovator. His methods were basically those of the Romans; it was his energy and general capacity that was remarkable. He is chiefly remembered as a great builder of bridges, canals and aqueducts rather than roads, but the Holyhead road, which he virtually rebuilt throughout its course, became perhaps the best road in Britain.

Roman roads were built for marching infantry and were paved with stone slabs. Such a surface is unsuitable for wheeled vehicles because gaps and changes in level are bound to develop between the slabs. A more flexible, continuous surface was required. The surface had to be hard enough so that wheels would not make ruts and yet rough enough to give a grip (modern metalled roads are not very suitable for horse-drawn vehicles because they are too smooth). Roads therefore consisted, ideally, of a very sound foundation and a surface layer of broken stone or gravel, which could be easily raked or scraped level when it became worn. Roads of this kind, though rare in England, are still to be found in thinly populated rural districts and are quite common in North America.

The most impressive roadbuilding of the first half of the eighteenth century was carried out in Scotland between 1726 and 1735 under the direction of General Wade. Like the Romans', General Wade's purpose was military, to suppress the Highland clans. Some of the roads and bridges commonly attributed to him were actually built later, though with the same purpose; altogether, about 800 miles of roads were constructed in the Highlands, all of them south of the line of the Caledonian Canal.

National defence has always commanded larger funds than social amenity; there was no comparable need for equivalent `programmes south of the Clyde and Forth, but the growth of wheeled traffic during the eighteenth century made roadbuilding and road improvement more and more urgent throughout the country. The dumping of earth or gravel on to the road in the hope that it would be knocked into a serviceable surface by the passing traffic was never a satisfactory procedure, and the heavier the traffic, the more obvious became the shortcomings of this method. In other European countries, notably France, roads were constructed with greater care, with several layers of large flat stones below the gravel surface and drainage ditches on either side.

Ironically, the first modern road engineer in England (the first to think in terms of making roads suitable for traffic rather than the other way round) was a blind man, John ('Blind Jack') Metcalfe of Knaresborough. This remarkable character, having lost his sight in early childhood, became a fearless horseman in pursuit of the fox, and a professional carter who drove his own wagon between Knaresborough and York. Among his acquaintances was Colonel Liddell, M.P for Berwick, who on one occasion offered him a lift from London to Harrogate in his coach. Metcalfe said he would rather walk. He did, and arrived in Harrogate a day earlier than the Colonel's coach.

In 1765 a trust was formed to build a turnpike from Harrogate to Boroughbridge, and Metcalfe decided to go into the roadmaking business. He persuaded the trustees to let him make three miles of new road, and finished the task with complete success in less than the usual time. Other jobs followed. At one time he was employing 400 men on a nine-mile stretch of road. His methods were basically the same as Telford was to adopt: a solid foundation, a gently arched surface of broken stone, and large ditches on either side. On one piece of road he was confronted with special problems. The swampy character of the area had defeated all previous road-making efforts. Metcalfe laid a foundation of heather twigs, covered by stone and gravel, and twelve years later this section of road was as good as new, although other parts of the same road had to be extensively repaired every year.

The total mileage of roads built by Metcalf was not large; but his work was important because he had grasped the two fundamental necessities of road building – good drainage and a sound foundation – which had been generally neglected hitherto. He was still building roads in the North of England in 1792, when he was seventy-five.

Of all the giants of the Industrial Revolution, Thomas Telford is perhaps the mightiest; at any rate, more survives of his work than of almost any other industrial architect and engineer. In his long and incredibly energetic life, roadbuilding was but one of his activities, and not the most notable, but he deserved the humorous title bestowed on him by his friend Southey, the 'Colossus of Roads'.

Telford was only eight years old when 'Blind Jack' Metcalfe began laying his first road. The only son of an Eskdale shepherd who died when the boy was a few months old, he was apprenticed to a stone-mason and, according to his biographer, L.T.C. Rolt, his mark can still be seen under the western arch of the Esk bridge at Langholm, on which he worked during his apprenticeship. At the age of twenty-four, like many another ambitious young Scot, he went to London to seek his fortune. He was armed with letters of introduction to, among others, Sir William Chambers, who employed him in the construction of Somerset House (the south-west corner of that building is Telford's handiwork).

Besides his natural skill, intelligence and ambition, Telford had an attractive personality, and he was seldom short of useful contacts. Sir William Pulteney sent him to superintend the restoration of Shrewsbury Castle, and he was soon appointed Surveyor of Public Works in the county. His career blossomed. Engineering had not yet became an acknowledged 'profession' (in later life Telford was to be the first president of the Institute of Civil Engineers), and he was archaeologist, architect and builder rolled into one. He was responsible for two churches in Shropshire, as well as his more famous and more numerous bridges. Between 1790 and 1796 he built forty bridges in the county, including the famous iron bridge at Buildwas, now, sad to say, no more. (The iron bridge at Coalbrookdale, happily preserved, predated and clearly influenced the Buildwas bridge, but the latter seems to have been technolgoically more advanced).

In 1793, Telford was appointed to the staff of the Ellesmere Canal Company, and he became, in fact if not in name, its chief designer and engineer. This massive project, especially Pont Cysylte, Telford's towering aqueduct over the Dee, made him a national celebrity. The aqueduct was not opened until 1805 and the canal not finished until three years later, but long before that, Telford, who had an astonishing capacity for doing six jobs at once, was engaged in other projects. He was appointed engineer to two Commissions to improve communications in the Highlands, based largely on the results of Telford's surveys. The first was for the Caledonian Canal and the second for Highland Roads and Bridges, which included ports and harbours.

There were no roads whatsoever in the northern Highlands in 1803, and the military roads of General Wade and his successors south of Inverness hardly served the needs of the people. Many of these roads had fallen into decay, as it was no longer likely that troops would have to be moved in to suppress a rising of the clans. The Highlanders had been crushed with brutal efficiency after Culloden, and the job was being finished off by the landlords who, having forgotten their clan loyalties with convenient speed, had, as Telford himself put it, "transferred their affections from the people to flocks of Sheep". The old black cattle were fast disappearing, and so were the crofters. The Western Highlands and Islands were in danger of complete depopulation.

The building of the Caledonian Canal has little to do with roads and coaching. That mighty project was completed at a rather greater cost than estimated and has been something of a white elephant ever since, though that is not Telford's fault. His road- and bridge-building scheme had further-reaching effects.

Engineers and architects whose names linger in the popular memory are usually remembered for one or two great works; with Telford, it is the Menai bridge or perhaps the Pont Cysyllte aqueduct. But, as Mr Rolt says, "Judged in terms of the sheer magnitude of the work involved and of its historical importance there can be no doubt that Telford's work in the Highlands was the greatest achievement of his career", and it "brought to the Highlands more lasting benefit than any project for Highland development, before or since".* The work took about twenty years and would never have been accomplished without

*A.R.B. Haldane

unstinting efforts in very difficult country, often in dangerous conditions, by Telford's six area surveyors and their teams. In all, nearly one thousand miles of roads were built, many of them through virgin territory, and over a thousand bridges. Besides this, Telford was responsible for nearly two hundred miles of roads in the Lowlands, including the road from Carlisle to Glasgow, a notorious stretch on which many a mail-coach had come to grief.

The making of the Holyhead road was an indirect result of the Act of Union with Ireland, which created a need for better communications between Dublin and London, especially for the Irish Members of Parliament who had to make the trip frequently. Holyhead-Howth was the shortest sea route, but it was not quick owing to poor land communications – the appalling state of the road in Anglesey, the necessity of crossing the Menai strait by ferry, and the rough, steep and indirect route through north Wales. In fact, the road was very poor for some distance east of Shrewsbury in the first decade of the nineteenth century. The mail went as far as Shrewsbury, and an attempt to put a mail-coach on the Shrewsbury-Holyhead road in 1808 had to be abandoned. The region was too thinly populated for the parish system of road maintenance to work. A multitude of turnpike trusts had responsibilities for the road – there were seventeen trusts between London and Shrewsbury – but they had not the means to undertake any restoration.

Telford was asked to survey the Shrewsbury-Holyhead road and the road from Bangor to Chester, and to advise on how a suitable mail-coach road might be built. He presented his conclusions in 1811 and, after the usual governmental delays, totalling five years in this instance, work began on the whole road from London to Holyhead. It was a huge project, not finally completed until the 1830s, although mail-coaches were running through to Holyhead long before that. West of Shrewsbury, the road was almost entirely new, and a major part of the London stretch was begun from scratch, shortening the distance and levelling the hills. At Telford's insistence, some trusts were bought out by the government, giving him full control. The cost was enormous: one stretch of about eighty miles was estimated by Telford at £53,000 a year for five years. The most expensive project was, of course, bridging the Menai strait, which Telford accomplished with his famous 579-foot suspension bridge, opened in 1826. The first vehicle to cross it was, appropriately, the London-Holyhead mail. A few months later, the Chester mail opened the Conway bridge on the Chester-Holyhead road, which connected the Midlands and North-West with the Irish steam packets at Holyhead. Telford celebrated his seventieth birthday in the same year, and though he had several years of activity left to him still, his road-building career was over.

Telford knew little theory and, like the Romans, he planned conservatively, preferring to err on the side of caution, with the result that his works have lasted and, given the chance, may well last as long as the Romans'. In building a road, he began by excavating and levelling. One of the chief drawbacks of military roads, General Wade's as well as the Romans', was that they included slopes too steep for horse-drawn traffic; Telford was determined to have easy gradients which, as most of his roads were in mountainous country, was not always easy to achieve. Nevertheless, the steepest slope on the Holyhead road, in the Nant Ffrancon Pass, was only 1:22. The actual structure of the road consisted of three layers, and could be roughly compared with the building of a house – foundation, walls and roof. The foundation consisted of interlocking large stones, broad end downwards, each stone not more than three inches wide at the top. On top and in between were laid smaller stones, "broken to about the size of walnuts", as Southey described them. The topmost layer was of smaller stones or coarse gravel; this was the least important layer and could even be omitted in certain circumstances. The basic principles were: a level surface; good drainage, provided by a slight camber, with cross-drains at regular intervals below the foundation leading to ditches on either side; and a firm substructure, capable of bearing the heaviest loads without being crushed or depressed.

Telford's roads were first-rate; no one questioned that. It was no coincidence that the first outstandingly fast day-coach of coaching's golden age, the Shrewsbury *Wonder*, ran on Telford's road. The only problem was that, for the average trust or highways commission, a Telford road was extremely expensive. There was no likelihood that the increased income from the improved or rebuilt road would balance the initial outlay. On most roads, therefore, the solution was not a mighty engineering feat on the Telford pattern, but macadamizing.

John Loudon McAdam was, like Telford, a Lowland Scot by birth, though he was of Highland descent. He was born, a year before Telford, into a small land-owning family then going through hard times which resulted in the loss of the family estate at Waterhead. As a boy he went to New York, where he had an uncle who was a prosperous merchant, in an effort to restore the family fortunes by trade. Whatever success he had – and he was treasurer of the New York Chamber of Commerce at eighteen – was lost during the American Revolution, and the story goes that he returned to Ayrshire a poor man. Something must have been salvaged somewhere, however, for McAdam was soon living in a large house and serving as deputy lieutenant of the county.

He travelled widely in the Lowlands during the 1780s, and was struck by the bad state of the roads. They were, he wrote, "at once loose, rough and perishable, expensive, dangerous to travel on and very costly to repair". With his cousin, the Earl of Dundonald, he laid down many miles of new roads in Ayrshire in the 1780s and 1790s, developing the methods that were to make his name famous.

In 1798, McAdam accepted a post as supplier to the navy in the west of England, and though this job lasted only until peace was signed three years later, he decided to settle in Bristol, at that time still the largest city in England after London. His methods of road improvement were already well-known, though it was not until 1816, when he was sixty years old, that he was appointed General Surveyor of the 146 miles of roads in the municipality of Bristol. Within a few years he was famous. He published his *Practical Essay on the Scientific Repair and Preservation of Roads* in 1819 and *The Present State of Road-Making* in 1820. He was asked to advise on road-building schemes all over England: in 1823 his son made a list of the trusts and parishes that had remade their roads according to the McAdam system; the total came to over seventy. J. L. McAdam played a prominent, and not uncontroversial, part in the parliamentary inquiry on road transport in 1823; finally, he was appointed General Surveyor of Roads for the whole kingdom in 1827. He was then well over seventy, and his sons, especially his second son, James, had taken over his work (in those days, engineers tended to form dynasties just like landowners; Telford, who never married, was an exception).

Telford disliked, and for the most part successfully avoided, acrimony. McAdam was a more combative character, who sometimes spoke his mind more plainly than was tactful. However, the Telford v. McAdam contest, though sometimes heated, was waged by their supporters, not by the two great engineers themselves (McAdam modestly disclaimed the title of 'engineer') who, oddly enough, did not know each other. McAdam's methods, unlike Telford's, aroused much criticism and even scorn. His biographer quotes a contemporary jingle:

> The Oxford Street natives fierce arguments raise
> About the best method of *mending their ways*:
> One party contending, 'midst loud altercation,
> That nothing will do but Macadamization;
> Another declares if their cash is to save meant,
> The road must be made o'er a hard stony pavement.

Though wrong about their relative economy, this sums up the difference between the McAdam method and the Telford method: in many respects they agreed, but where they differed was in their attitude to the foundation. McAdam denied that the solid basis of large stones was necessary, or even desirable. Providing the road was well drained and made of the right materials, said McAdam, it needed no artificial foundation. He was very particular about the size of the stones used. They should not be more than one inch across or six ounces in weight. Eventually, his workmen were provided with a ring, which the stones had to pass through, or a small scale to weigh them, but in the early days McAdam told his men to see if they could get a doubtful stone in their mouths: if not, it was too big. There is a story that McAdam was once inspecting a newly laid road and was annoyed to observe that many of the stones were too big. He approached the workman responsible and inquired, none too politely, why he was using stones of the wrong size. The man turned to answer and McAdam immediately understood the reason for the mistake. Nature had given the man a mouth like a post box, the vast capacity of which was further enlarged by a total absence of teeth.

A properly laid road, ten inches thick and raised above the general level of the ground, would support any traffic, said McAdam. A foundation of hefty stones offered no advantage and could be a positive drawback for, if it shifted, it would allow pockets of water to collect, undermining the road. He went so far as to say that he preferred to build a road on soft soil than on hard natural rock, which offered no elasticity and would cause the road to wear our more quickly.

Apart from this fundamental difference, McAdam and Telford's ideas about roadmaking were not dissimilar. They both understood the importance of using small, uniform stones, free from sand or soil, which would be ground by iron-shod wheels into a hard, waterproof surface. Probably neither of them fully understood the theory of this – that owing to surface tension, rainwater actually helps to cement the tiny particles of stone together. It works for iron tyres, which grind the stones and pack the gritty particles together; it would not work for pneumatic tyres, which suck up the grit and create dust or mud; an effect that was to be overcome by adding a sealing agent such as tar.

Although some stubborn souls continued to pour scorn on McAdam's ideas long after his roads had proved themselves, his method was incomparably cheaper than Telford's and was the method generally employed. McAdam and his almost equally peripatetic sons did not of course supervise the rebuilding of every road in the country, though they were directly involved with an enormous number. But McAdam's system soon became universal: virtually every major road, not to mention city streets, was 'macadamized' by about 1835.

To the public, McAdam became a sort of half-humorous, 'superman' figure. He was the subject of numerous jokes and cartoons; the verb 'macadamize' passed rapidly into the language, and was used by poets in some highly incongruous senses (a music critic wrote of 'macadamized sounds'). McAdam was, naturally, a particular hero of coachmen and of all who travelled frequently by road; Nimrod called him, "next to Dr Jenner, the greatest contributor to the welfare of mankind that this country has ever produced".

Hardly less important than McAdam's reform of roadbuilding methods was his advocacy of new means of administration. His travels up and down the kingdom had shown him the inadequacy of the trusts and the undesirability of statute labour. He advocated parliamentary control of the trusts and the appointment of well-trained and adequately paid surveyors. Largely as a result of his and his sons' urging, some consolidation of trusts under a single authority was effected, with a resulting increase in efficiency and decline in expenditure. The trend would undoubtedly have continued if the arrival of railways had not once more relegated the roads to a lowly place among national priorities. McAdam, who died in 1836, did not live to see his work abandoned before the encroaching rails.

NINE

Coaching Business

Not many people made large fortunes operating a coaching business, and the small group of proprietors in London and the provinces who really were rich often had other interests, sometimes unconnected with coaching. Edward Sherman was a stockbroker before he took over the Bull and Mouth, and he could often be seen in a tavern next to the stock exchange chatting to his City friends. His three successive marriages to elderly widows also contributed to his fortune. Such assets were to be invaluable when, in the first two years after the opening of the London-Birmingham railway, Sherman's coaching business suffered the swingeing loss of £7,000.

The rapid expansion of coaching in the 1820s and 1830s made more bankrupts than millionaires. The little men were rapidly forced out of business, and the major lines fell into the hands of a few large proprietors like Sherman. Coaching was a complicated business which required capital, a substantial number of employees, and reliable sub-contractors, over whom the proprietor had little direct control. Except on a few routes, profit margins were small, and the risks were considerable.

The route of a mail- or stage-coach was known as the 'ground', and was roughly divided into three: the upper ground (the part closest to London), the middle ground, and the lower ground (the part nearest the provincial terminus). Thus, one went 'up' to London and 'down' to the country, as one still does when travelling by train or car. The journey was more precisely divided into stages, where the horses were changed. The length of a stage varied, depending on the availability of horses, the nature of the ground, and the scheduled speed of the coach – slow coaches required fewer changes. The average length of a stage was eight to ten miles, seldom less than five or more than fifteen. On the Brighton road via Lewes, six teams were used, changing at intervals of ten miles, nine, ten, thirteen, eight, and eight. Brighton coaches that went via Horsham managed with one change fewer, but that road was a mile or two shorter. On the Bath road, changes were more frequent, at any rate on the lower ground between Newbury and Bath where the longest stage was only seven miles. Stages tended to be longer on long routes: the average stage for a London-Edinburgh stage-coach in 1832 was fourteen miles.

By the 1820s, most coaches, mail and stage, conformed more or less closely to a recognizable type, but because there were as many coachbuilders as there were coach proprietors, superficial variations were numerous, especially as each proprietor tried to make his own vehicles as noticeable as possible – hence the sometimes garish appearance of stage-coaches on which De Quincey commented disdainfully. In some cases the difference went deeper than paint. A number of odd-looking 'safety' coaches were introduced at different times, incorporating various more or less successful devices to reduce the risk of overturning, while some proprietors favoured different styles. Edward Sherman, though among the three largest coach proprietors in London in the 1830s, preferred his coaches built in an old-fashioned style that was otherwise only seen on remote cross-country roads. As they were usually painted a bright yellow, Sherman's coaches at least had the merit of being easily recognised.

The coach proprietor ordered his coaches from a coachbuilder, specifying the design and decoration he required. As a rule he did not own the vehicles but hired them from the builder, who was also responsible for maintaining them, as Vidler built and maintained the mail-coaches for the Post Office. The charge for hire was usually about 3d a double mile (i.e. one mile of the route there and back or, in coaching language, 'both sides of the ground').

Some proprietors bought their coaches outright and some built their own because there happened to be a coachbuilding concern connected with their coaching business. For instance,

Mrs Mountain at the Saracen's Head in Holborn (where Nicholas Nickleby set out for Yorkshire with Mr Squeers) had a coachbuilder's workshop on her premises. She ran the Louth mail as well as several stage-coaches in partnership with others, and rented her coaches, which cost about £120 to build, to the syndicate of which she was a member at the charge of 3½d per double mile. (Sherman also owned a coachbuilding business, though some of his coaches were hired from other builders.)

Barring accidents, Mrs Mountain ought to have made her money back on each coach in less than a year, but her construction costs were lower than average while her hiring charges were higher. What with repairing damaged or worn-out parts, most coachbuilders probably had to wait nearer two years before they saw a return on their initial outlay. According to Nimrod, the cost of building a stage-coach in about 1830 was £130 – £150, but this must have varied considerably according to the degree of luxury required for the interior. There were no frills for a slow coach on an unfashionable route, but one of Sherman's crack coaches had mounted inside a timetable carved in ivory, which was illuminated at night by a reflecting lamp.

Each route demanded several coaches. Four was the desirable minimum for a daily route of about one hundred miles – an 'up' coach and a 'down' coach plus a spare vehicle at either end in case of breakdown. Thus, the Shrewsbury *Wonder* or the Birmingham *Tally-Ho* was not a single vehicle but merely one of the coaches that ran a certain route. To complicate matters, the same names were frequently used on different routes and, in the case of the *Tally-Ho* among others, by rival proprietors on the same route.

The chief structural advance made in the coaches of the 1820s and 1830s was the improvement in springs, which allowed a curved and slender perch – or indeed no perch at all. The body could thus be suspended nearer the ground, making the coach less top-heavy and permitting rather more head-room. As late as the 1830s most coaches were still without proper brakes, largely because the coachbuilders disapproved of them. They tended to wear out quickly and placed an additional strain on the wheels always the most vulnerable parts. In the absence of a Ralph Nader, the safety of the public continued to depend on the strength of the wheelers (the pair of horses nearest the coach) and, on steep hills, the application of a drag to the rear wheels.

The improvement of roads made brakes all the more necessary simply because a smooth surface offered less resistance than a rough one, and from the late 1820s some of the mails at least were fitted with a simple screw-down clamp, operated by the guard. It saved him from the tiresome and dangerous task of jumping off the coach to lodge a 'shoe' under the wheel, but was otherwise hardly less crude a method of retarding the coach. Ten years later a more sophisticated brake, operated by the coachman's foot as in an automobile, was coming into use, but that was like building a better balloon in the year the Wright brothers took off.

Coach proprietors were almost invariably innkeepers, and the great London proprietors worked out of more than one inn. An inn provided the ideal base – food and lodging for passengers, stabling for the horses, with ticket office, waiting room and porters all at hand. Usually, a coach service was started by a partnership, each member contributing a share of the costs and taking a proportionate share of the profits. Indeed, it was virtually impossible for a coachmaster to be completely independent, because his service relied so heavily on the co-operation of others in distant parts of the country. A London proprietor would run his coach in partnership with a colleague who lived at the other end of the route, and some kind of agreement was made by the two of them with all those along the route who provided the horses. As a rule, the London proprietor would horse the coach for the first stage only, or the first two stages; large numbers of horses were kept by the big London proprietors at such places as Barnet, where William Horne had two hundred horses stabled, and Hounslow, where William Chaplin had twice as many, these being the first staging points on important roads out of London. Thereafter, the fresh horses would normally be provided by innkeepers and others along the road. There were exceptions: Sherman horsed a Birmingham night coach as far as Daventry (seventy-odd miles), though the number of fresh horses required for this particular coach was probably not very large.

The horsing of the coach was the most expensive and the most problematical part of the business, for the proprietors, no matter how great a figure they cut in London or Liverpool, were at the mercy of the country innkeepers who contracted to keep their coaches on the move. In thinly populated areas, there was little choice in the matter, and a man who knew that there was no one else in the vicinity who could provide daily teams of fresh horses held a very strong position in any argument with the proprietor. This type of difficulty was less likely to arise if all those horsing the coach had a stake in the profits, so it made sense to give the country innkeepers a share in the business.

Country contractors naturally varied in the efficiency with which they horsed the coach. Some very strange beasts were provided for night runs, when darkness prevented too close an inspection by the coachman. (Horses that had been acquired by devious means were also reserved for night duty, when they were unlikely to be recognized). Harry Salisbury, who drove the *Tantivy* between Oxford and Birmingham, was always complaining about the quality of the horses provided at Stratford-on-Avon. The whole team was not worth £25, said Harry, and he reckoned that they had probably been owned by Shakespeare.

It was the middle ground that presented the greatest difficulties, especially for the mails which, leaving London at 8 p.m., travelled over the middle ground in the middle of the night. An innkeeper or his horsekeeper was reluctant to turn out at 1 a.m. or 2 a.m. just to change a team of horses. Fast coaches, moreover, seldom stopped long enough for the passengers to buy a drink, and the country innkeeper was tempted to create delays deliberately in order to do some trade in the bar. His posting customers were more rewarding, and he was inclined to keep the best horses for them, palming off second-rate animals on the coach. Such conflicts of interest between city proprietor and country contractor could be overcome, or at any rate reduced, if the country men had a stake in the coach's profit.

Besides the country innkeepers, local landowners sometimes contracted to horse a coach that passed through their area. When coaching became a fashionable hobby after the Napoleonic wars, some high-sounding names were to be found listed among the partners in coaching concerns and, indeed, among the coachmen themselves. A gentleman who undertook to horse a stage-coach did so for reasons of prestige and personal satisfaction and was unlikely to provide broken-down horses, though there might be other disadvantages in a business connection with the gentry.

The qualities required in coach horses were not particularly unusual and, conveniently, were not precisely the same as those required for other purposes. For example, a vicious horse might be impossible to ride but, harnessed with three other horses in a team, he would usually settle down and perform perfectly. Other faults that might have been regarded as serious disabilities in other circumstances were no particular drawback in coach horses. A remarkably large number was blind. Blindness obviously did not matter much in wheelers, but it was not unusual among leaders also. Colonel Corbett remembered a blind leader on the Shrewsbury *Greyhound* which, "if he had been all right, would have commanded at least a hundred guineas for a gentleman's carriage. . . . He quite won my heart by the high couraged manner in which he elbowed his way through the large droves of cattle which were being driven along the road from Shrewsbury fair". Nimrod tells the story of a one-eyed coachman who, after crossing a tricky bridge with success, boasted that he and his team had only one eye among the lot of them.

Buying a coach horse was always something of a risk, as there were some that just would not go in harness. When he was driving a coach on the Oxford road, Thomas Cross sometimes undertook to buy horses on behalf of his London employer in Oxford, where they were cheaper.

One afternoon a tout, or man who was a sort of horse-dealer's cad, came and told me, as a great favour, of a horse that was to be disposed of for a little money. I went with him, and was shown a very useful coach horse. I asked to see him out. This was complied with, and, running my eye over him, and approving his action, I said, "Sound?"

"Perfectly; but I don't warrant him."

"Age?"

"Six years old."

Looking in his mouth, I found this to be correct,

"Price?" I said.

"Ten pounds", was the reply.

I immediately concluded something was wrong, as he looked like a five-and-thirty pounds' horse.

"He's not a kicker?" I said.

"You can't make him kick", was the reply.

I was almost ashamed to say, "You won't warrant him quite, I suppose?"

"You can't expect it, at that price; but all I have told you is true".

"Then, I'll have him", I said.

I observed a titter on the lips of the stablemen as I followed him into the house to give him the money, when the seller candidly told me that he had given thirty pounds for the horse, and had sold him two or three times for more money; but he had always been returned, as he would not go in harness. Not very well satisfied with my bargain, I walked away, desiring him to send the horse round to the 'Roebuck'.

Early in the next morning I borrowed a break, harnessed him, and put him to with another horse, but he would not move; and, touching him with the whip, he reared right on end, then threw himself down, and there lay. At this I scratched my head, and thought it was a bad case, when my friend who had kindly put me up to this great bargain called to me and said, "Master, master, light a truss of straw and put it under him!" Nothing loth to make a trial of such a remedy, as I had heard of it before, though I had never seen it practised, and there not being many people about, as it was early in the morning, we unbuckled his traces, got him out, and with the other horse drew the break out in the corn market, and put him to again, as I was not to be beaten without a further trial. My friend, therefore, procured me a wisp of straw, and strewed it on the ground under him, and when I was ready set fire to it; the animal made two or three plunges clear of the straw, and then threw himself down.

Satisfied now that he might be made to go, but not by such means, I thought I would try another element which I had before seen applied with success. After getting him up, I had him taken down to the canal, where I found a barge just going to start with two horses at length; giving the bargeman 2s 6d to lend me some draught harness, with his permission we put him in behind the other two, first taking the precaution to have the barge moored clear of the quay and other craft. We then moved on, when the brute threw himself about – first up in the air – then down on his knees – up again – then forward – then back on his haunches; but the two fore horses kept on, and their traces, acting upon the barge, did not give him time to lay down, and, after two or three attempts to baffle us, he rolled off the towing-path into the canal.

The recalcitrant horse was displeased by his soaking, however, and decided to surrender; Cross later drove him regularly on a twelve-mile stage, "and no horse ever went better or quieter"

Individual idiosyncrasies often disappeared when a horse was harnessed in a team, but horses could not be arbitrarily harnessed together. Each pair had to be well matched physically. Unequal strides would soon set the coach rocking and make the coachman's job more difficult. This was particularly important for the wheelers, the powerhouse of the team, who had to check the coach on downward slopes as well as propel it along the level. The wheelers were usually the better pair, for they did the most work, yet in some respects the leaders were more vital. If one of the wheelers packed up, a good coachman could 'carry' it, but if a leader broke down he was stuck.

The whole subject of coach horses, like everything to do with horses in England, is a complex and fascinating mass of folklore, craftsmanship and earthy wisdom. Much of it is explained in the tangy pages of Nimrod (C.J. Apperley), an experienced amatuer coachman who also horsed a coach named after him on the Southampton road at one time.

For the sake of a dashing appearance, the proprietors of the smartest coaches sometimes tried to match their teams in looks. One Sussex coachmaster with three piebalds and a grey is said to have painted the grey to match its team mates. In the annual procession of the mails on the king's birthday, all Sherman's mail-coaches were drawn by black horses; but for daily business few coach proprietors could be so particular. A man named Taylor who horsed the Holyhead mail for two stages near Shrewsbury had a team of bays, a team of greys, and two teams of chestnuts, and the ultra-smart Windsor *Taglioni* had a team of piebalds, but for the most part it was only private owners who paid attention to such details. The well-known gentleman-coachman, Sir Henry Peyton, drove greys exclusively and so did another enthusiast, Colonel Sibthorpe, the reactionary M.P. for Lincolnshire.

Odd characteristics in a horse (Lord Algernon St Maur knew a grey leader at Hounslow that would not go without ear caps) and minor faults of temperament or senses might be disregarded, but coach horses had to be in good general condition. A coachmaster who tried to cut his costs by buying cheap horses would not stay in business for long. At the best of times, the working life of a coach horse was appallingly short – about three years on a fast coach – and second-rate animals would not last the pace for more than a few weeks. In spite of Hogarth's graphic protests, only a few people were yet deeply concerned about cruelty to animals, but too many horses dropping dead in their traces soon earned a coach a bad reputation.

Once a coach horse was worn out, it was not necessarily disqualified for other purposes which did not require it to trot ten miles twice a day at more than a furlong a minute and harnessed to a vehicle weighing as much as two tons. The coachmaster might therefore get a few pounds on his original purchase by selling retired horses to a local farmer.

A remarkable display of stamina by coach horses was shown by a team that had just been released at the end of its stage on the Liverpool mail in February, 1807. Hearing the sound of a fox hunt, the horses set off after it, still in their collars and harness. "One of them," says Lord William Pitt Lennox, "a blood mare, kept the track with the whipper-in, and gallantly followed him for about two hours, over every leap he took, until the fox, who was a cowardly rogue, had led them round in a ring fence, and ran to ground. . . . These spirited horses were led back to the inn at Monk's Heath, and performed their stage back to Congleton the same evening, apparently in higher spirits for having had a gallop with the hounds."

For the fashionable fast coaches, the ideal was one horse per double mile (each horse working three days out of four), and although the number was invariably less than that in practice, it can be seen that a very large number of horses was involved in the coaching business. The purchase (or hire) and maintenance of the horses thus made up the largest item of expenditure in running a coach.

A sound horse could sometimes be purchased for as little as ten guineas, owing to some fault that disqualified it for other purposes, but the average price was twenty-five or thirty guineas and, on a first-class fast coach, the team might be worth three hundred pounds or more. A private owner in Oxfordshire was prepared to pay 300 guineas for a single coach horse.

The cost of keeping a horse varied enormously in different parts of the country. Nimrod reckoned it at about four pounds a month, including the wages of horsekeepers and stablehands, but it was probably less than that in country districts. Colonel Corbett quoted a figure of 17s 6d a week, "including blacksmith", but saddler, vet., and "depreciation" extra.

Wages for the coachman and guard (if any) were a relatively small item, largely because wages were so low. A coachman was

paid about double the miserly half-guinea earned weekly by the
mail-coach guard but, like the guard, he derived more of his
income from tips than from wages. Tipping was generous and so
conventional that, from the passenger's point of view, it
represented a virtual surcharge on the fare – another reason why
people preferred to travel on the railways. The coachman also
made a few shillings from passengers whom he picked up and
carried for a short distance without entering their names on the
waybill. Coach proprietors often connived at this custom, which
was known as 'shouldering'.

The expenses that the coach proprietors found most irritating,
especially during their short-lived rivalry with the lightly taxed
railways, were government duties and licenses. These duties were
calculated according to the number of passengers the coach could
carry, not on the number who actually travelled, so that the same
mileage charge was levied on an empty coach – known in the
colourful language of the road as a 'crazy woman' – as on a full
one. The mileage duty on each stage-coach was about 3d a mile,
depending on the number of passengers the coach was licensed to
carry. Coach proprietors often licensed their coaches for a smaller
number of passengers in the winter, when custom declined, than
in the summer, and so saved themselves a few pounds.

In addition, there was a road tax for keeping each vehicle on
the road, regardless of how often it ran, and a tax on each
coachman and guard, regardless of how often they were
employed. These duties added up to a hefty item in the
proprietor's expenditure: in the year 1835, the duties and tax paid
on the *Wellington* coach from London to Newcastle, licensed to
carry four inside and eleven outside, came to a total of
£2,568 18s 6d.

Besides these governmental duties, the stage-coach had to pay
tolls on the turnpikes. According to Stanley Harris, a large
London proprietor might find himself paying as much as 11s 6d
per mile each month under this head. The tolls paid by the
Wellington in 1835 almost equalled the duties – £2,537 7s 8d.
These two items, plus the hire of coaches (£1,274) brought the
total cost of running this coach, not counting wages of staff or
keep of horses, to over £6,000 per annum. The maximum
number of passengers that the coach could carry in a year,
assuming 364 double journeys with never an empty seat, was
10,920. The fares were £4 10s inside and £2 5s outside, giving a

theoretical maximum income of £31,122. But no coach regularly carried the maximum number of passengers: the thirty coaches that passed through the Shenfield tollgate on 28th February 1838, carried seventy-seven inside passengers, though the number of seats available, even if none had more than four inside, was 120. The annual gross income from fares on the *Wellington*, therefore, was probably not more than £25,000 and, as this particular coach was reduced from seven to six days a week in the following year as a result of falling custom, may well have been much lower. At any rate, probably at least one quarter of the total receipts was immediately swallowed by taxes, tolls and coach hire.

The costs of horsing are not easy to calculate, partly because they varied in different parts of the country (a London coachmaster complained that a colleague beyond Stamford could horse a coach for half of what he had to pay) and partly because they were divided among the partners or sub-contractors participating in the service. Accounts for the Bristol mail in the month of December 1839, published by Stanley Harris in *The Coaching Age*, show that the rate paid to the contractors was £4 14s for six and a half miles, though one man received a slightly lower rate on one stretch.

With these costs, travel by coach could never be cheap. Fares varied considerably in different regions and on journeys of various lengths, but the figure of 5d a mile, often quoted as an average price, gives an idea of the costliness of journeys by coach, and on the mails and the crack stage-coaches the average fare was higher. A seat on the outside cost half or slightly more than half the inside fare, on average about 3d a mile, and as a result coaches were sometimes crowded on the outside while the inside seats were unoccupied.

A successful coach had to earn not less than £4 (Nimrod says £5) per double mile per month. Some failed to reach that figure, but others exceeded it comfortably, earning as much as £6 or £8. The fastest, most fashionable coaches were not on the whole the most profitable, owing to the greater cost and shorter working lives of the horses. But they were the coaches that were known and remembered, and so they were often run at a loss for the sake of the renown they brought to their proprietors, who financed the deficits out of the earnings of their more profitable but less glamorous slow coaches.

Besides the high running costs of the business, the coach

proprietor had to allow for a variety of occupational hazards, some natural, some commercial. When accidents occurred, the proprietors of the coach were held liable for damages where negligence could be proved, and most accidents happened, partly at least, as a result of carelessness. Serious accidents frequently cost the proprietors substantial settlements of damages, and even minor mishaps were sometimes relatively expensive. When the Edinburgh-Glasgow stage-coach was overturned in March 1839, the hat of one of the passengers was destroyed, or lost, or damaged beyond repair. In compensation the company paid 23s 6d, which prompted Stanley Harris to remark that the hat "must have been a first-rate new beaver". Damages for physical injury were naturally on a different scale. A sympathetic jury awarded £400 to a young girl who had sustained a broken arm and other injuries when the coach in which she was travelling overturned. In 1813 a man sued the proprietors of a mail-coach after suffering a compound fracture of the leg in an overturn, and was awarded £600.

Whether or not these accidents were the fault of the driver, an incompetent or irresponsible coachman could be a grave liability to his employers. Nimrod quotes one case — admittedly, he says, the only one he knew — of a coach company that successfully sued its own coachman for careless driving and won £100. He must have been more affluent than the average coachman — if he paid up.

When a coach started on a new route, it soon became evident to interested observers whether or not it was a paying proposition. If it were seen to be prospering, then almost certainly a rival company would appear on the ground, forcing sharp competition including price-cutting, and thus severely restricting profits. Many roads were busy enough to allow several companies to operate profitably, but the competitive free-for-all that was ferociously fought out on some routes benefitted neither the proprietors nor the passengers, for whom fare reductions did not compensate for the fear, discomfort and possible harm they suffered through the determination of a coachman to beat his rival's time.

On the heavily travelled Brighton road during the 1820s, several companies were losing amounts of fifty pounds and more a week as they slashed their prices in half in an effort to undercut competitors. A few, as William Blew says, "galloped straight into the Bankruptcy Court". The remaining proprietors eventually came to a sensible agreement and fares were restored to an economical level.

No coach was immune from this kind of competition. Sherman's famous Shrewsbury *Wonder*, which for thirteen years covered the ground between Shrewsbury and the capital with such punctuality that the villagers along the route reputedly set their watches by it, was threatened by a rival, travelling the same road through to Holyhead, which departed just ahead of it. Sherman and his partners retaliated by introducing a second coach, schedule to run in front of the newcomer which, with the *Wonder* running close behind it, was thus neatly bracketed. It is said that all three coaches sometimes arrived in London at the same time. When this pressure did not repel the intruder, the fares on the *Wonder* were cut to a point at which its proprietors were suffering a loss of nearly one hundred pounds a month. But it was the railway that eventually accomplished what rival coaches failed to do, and the *Wonder* in its last year endured the indignity of travelling part of the ground in a railway truck.

Such battles were not fought out in silence. Old-established companies resorted to the columns of the press to call upon the loyalty of their customers, while new competitors retaliated with descriptions of the superiority of the new service. John Copeland quotes the following example of propaganda issued during a contest on the Ipswich road in 1834.

> Stimulated by exertion by a determined opposition, the proprietors of the Magnet coach are prepared to meet the crisis with the weight of superior forces, and the support of a more extensive connection. They are grateful for past favours, and will continue to deserve them by one firm undeviating line of conduct. Passengers will receive the most marked attention and accommodation. Parcels will be delivered with the utmost determined promptitude, and the coach times with the utmost punctuality.

The announcement is worthy of a political speech writer: all it says is that the service will continue in the usual (efficient) manner. Although a small reduction in fares did follow, clearly the rivalry here was nothing like as intense as it was, for instance, on the Huddersfield-Manchester road in the summer of 1836, when the fare was announced as "Outside, what you please, inside, ditto".

The names of some coaches reflected the determination of their proprietors to deal briskly with opposition. The *Defiance, Spitfire,* and *Revenge* expressed an aggressive spirit similar to that encouraged by some automobile manufacturers nowadays; no doubt the passengers felt a certain sense of incongruity at riding in such fiercely characterised vehicles, just as the suburban housewife must feel rather odd driving decorously to the shops in a car labelled *Avenger* or *Fury.* But, as yet, Ford and Chrysler have not attempted to appease the competitive drive of their rivals as some coachmasters did in the nineteenth century by giving their vehicles names such as *Fair Play, Good Intent* and *Live-and-let-live.*

One item of expenditure that figures less prominently in the accounts of the coaching companies than in those of their modern counterparts was advertizing. Nevertheless, they did advertize, and many interesting coaching bills, once pasted on walls and fences, have survived. As the East Anglian example quoted above shows, the authors of coaching advertisements could write flannel just as effectively as their descendants in Madison Avenue and elsewhere.

Another method of advertising adopted especially by the London coachmasters, and still seen occasionally today, was the sandwich board. For a shilling or two, a man could be hired to stroll up and down the city streets bearing, back and front, the news of improvements or alterations in travel arrangements. Some proprietors had small handbills printed on coloured paper bearing a superficial resemblance to banknotes and containing a promise to convey the bearer to the relevant destination on payment of whatever sum corresponded to the fare. These were handed out to likely customers at coaching inns.

Stage-coaches were strictly controlled – persecuted, some proprietors said – by the government. The number of passengers they might carry, even the height to which luggage might be piled on the roof – these details were regulated by Act of Parliament, and substantial fines were levied on those convicted of infringements. Edward Sherman found it necessary in 1840 to issue a printed notice to his coachmen reminding them that "this coach is licensed to carry four inside and nine outside; and if more be carried either inside or outside, the proprietors forfeit five pounds, and the driver also five pounds, for each passenger

16. Pollard's view of the new G.P.O. in St Martin's-le-Grand, with the old Bull and Mouth in the background. With his usual meticulous accuracy, the artist has filled the foreground with a selection of hackney cabs as seen in London in the 1830s.

17. John Loudon McAdam. "By his indefatigable exertions, and his success as a roadmaker, by greatly saving animal labour, facilitating commercial intercourse, and rendering travelling easy and expeditious, he entitled himself to the reputation of a public benefactor' (Samuel Smiles).

18. Telford's masterpiece, the suspension bridge over the Menai Straits. When completed in 1826, it was the world's longest suspension bridge.

19, 20, 21. (*Above*) the York mail preserved in the Science Museum, London. Though bearing Queen Victoria's monogram, it was built in 1820 and is one of the few surviving vehicles of its type (no pre-Victorian stage-coach is known to exist. (*Left*) Mr Tomlinson, a humble provincial proprietor who also drove the coach, a more typical figure than the great William Chaplin (*below*).

22. Rowlandson's view of a horse sale in London. The business in horses can be compared, not too fancifully, with the business in cars today, and horse dealers knew as many tricks as the most devious second-hand-car salesman.

23. Stage-coaches racing, after C. Cooper Henderson. A couple of stone breakers in the foreground contemplate the sport.

24. "The Overset", Rowlandson's lively watercolour of a coach overturning. Contemporaries were shocked by the frequency of coaching
accidents, but those accustomed to motorcar mayhem may find their
concern merely quaint (*Reproduced by gracious permission of Her Majesty
the Queen*).

25. "The Result of Feather-Edging" (cutting corners), a lithograph
published in Captain Malet's *Annals of the Road.*

26. A stage-coach changing horses, after a painting by Cooper Henderson.

27. "Stage-coachmen at the Golden Fleece, Brighton", a drawing by J. and G. Temple published in W. C. A. Blew *Brighton and Its Coaches*.

28. James Pollard's well-known picture of coach passengers taking breakfast at the Bull Inn, Redbourn, 1831. One gentleman is getting a shave, another is changing his boots. One coachman, having completed his stint, duns the passengers, others hog the fire, while outside a guard sounds his horn, advising the passengers to hurry.

29. The yard of the Bull and Mouth.

30. The Brighton "Age", with Stevenson on the box, outside the West-End ticket office of the Bull and Mouth.

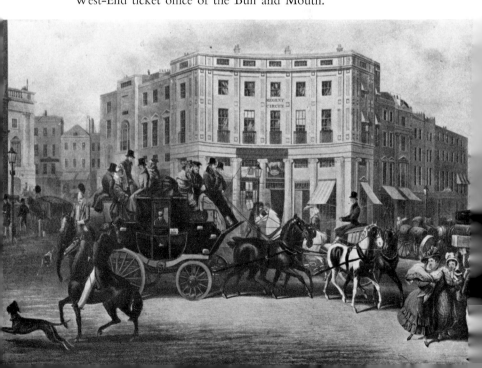

more than the number". Further details followed and the notice ended on a faint note of desperation: "There are many other regulations, for the neglect of which penalties are imposed, and as to which it is necessary that all parties concerned should consult the Act of Parliament".

Not surprisingly, such regulations were often broken. A coachman with his legal maximum load found it hard to resist the temptation, whether for his own gain or out of compassion, to pick up a solitary traveller on the road, especially if his coach happened to be licensed at that time for a smaller number of passengers than it normally carried in busier times. Yet it was a risky act, because should one of his passengers be annoyed with him, or merely excessively law-abiding, the infringement would be reported.

There were some not very pleasant characters about who made a living of a sort as informers against coaches (they received a share of the fine for reporting a coach that broke the rules). Every coachman in the Brighton area knew, by reputation at least, an informer called Byers, a name that their employers frequently cursed. Byers began his career as an agent for another informer, in which capacity he was instrumental in bringing several coach proprietors to book for carrying too many passengers, not having their names painted on the coach door, and similar misdemeanors. Encouraged by his success with the Brighton magistrates, Byers branched out on his own and wisely quit Brighton, where he had made himself so unpopular with many prominent citizens, for greener pastures in Bath. Within two weeks in November, 1825, he reported no less than 34 coaching irregularities, which cost the Bath coachmasters £500 plus costs. After this profitable raid in the west, the informer went to ground for a time.

In the summer of 1827 Byers reappeared in Brighton with at least one informer, a man named Rolland, now working for him. This time he was rather less successful. He gained £2 10s (half the fine from the prosecution of a van driver who had failed to show on his van the number of passengers he was licensed to carry), and £5 from a coach owner who had overloaded his coach; but another case, in which a coach was said to have driven a horseman off the road, was dismissed, and a coach proprietor whom Byers had accused of carrying too many passengers was able to prove that the coach was on its way to a funeral at the time and not carrying farepaying passengers.

Soon after this Byers was arrested for debt; perhaps his peculiar profession was not, after all, a very profitable one. But it did require certain talents – a thick skin, perseverance, and considerable ingenuity in discovering minute breaches of the letter of the law. One man who worked for Byers later changed sides and set himself up as a technical expert who, for a fee, represented coach proprietors at legal hearings. In this capacity he once confronted, and defeated, his old employer in a London law court.

All these incidental liabilities – fines for infringing regulations, compensation to victims of accidents and minor unbudgeted expenses of numerous kinds – on top of all the ordinary hazards of operation, made coaching too risky a business for the small, independent operator. Coaches were thus usually run by partnerships which, on the major routes in the 1820s and 1830s, were dominated by one of the great London proprietors.

The name of Edward Sherman has cropped up already. He took over the Bull and Mouth in St Martin's-le-Grand in 1823, and also operated from the Oxford Arms, Newgate, where his main business was freight. Most of his coaches ran to the north and north-west; at his prime, shortly before the opening of the railway, he had no less than nine coaches daily to Birmingham. His speciality was the fast day-coach. The aptly named Shrewsbury *Wonder* was begun by Sherman in 1825, and he later opened a one-day service to Manchester, 186 miles away, with the *Telegraph*. The London-Newcastle *Wellington*, the accounts of which are quoted above, was a Sherman coach, and he had a virtual monopoly of the Scottish mails. A familiar figure with his large moustache and shaved chin (then an unusual combination), driving his yellow chaise with a 'tiger' (an exquisitely turned-out pageboy) up behind, Sherman had the reputation of being a hard, indeed a mean, man to do business with. According to Stanley Harris, Sherman would make a small charge against his partners for the straw he provided to keep the passengers' feet warm, and he charged slightly higher than average rates for the coaches he owned. Country innkeepers sharing in his business put up with these small impositions for the sake of the connection with the Bull and Mouth, the busiest of all the great London coaching inns.

Sherman's chief rival was Benjamin Worthy Horne, who was concerned in launching the rival coach on the Shrewsbury road that tried to drive the *Wonder* out of business. Horne had three coaching inns, the best known of them the Golden Cross in what is now Trafalgar Square, but none of them as famous as the Bull and Mouth. He inherited the business from his father, William, who died in his forties supposedly as a result of overwork. The younger Horne was as tough a businessman as Sherman. He once drove a rival coach off the road by the simple expedient of buying up all the available horses at a certain stage. Horne horsed five of the London mails to the south and west, some of them in partnership with other London coachmasters, and his best-known stage-coaches were the Liverpool *Umpire*, the Bedford *Times* (very fast) and the *Independent Tally-Ho* to Birmingham, one of at least three 'Tally-Ho' coaches on that ground. With the coming of the railways, which ruined so many in the coaching business, Horne recognised that his business was doomed, and was quick to save himself by buying an interest in the London and Birmingham railway. Here he entered into partnership with another quick-thinking London coachmaster, the greatest of them all, William Chaplin.

By the standards of the 1830s, Chaplin's business was huge. He had no less than five coaching inns in London, owned or leased. The best known was the Swan With Two Necks in Lad Lane, north of Cheapside. Altogether, he stabled some 1400 horses in London and another 400 at Hounslow. He employed nearly 2,000 people and used 200 coaches on sixty or seventy lines. Half the mails that left London every night were horsed by him, including the *Quicksilver* Devonport and the Bristol mail, the earliest of them all.

Chaplin, born in 1787, was the son of a coachman and began his working life in the same trade. By dint of a sharp business sense, great energy, and an attractive personality, he became the largest coach proprietor in the country, M.P. for Salisbury, and director of two railway companies. He was well liked by his employees, from crack coachman to humble stableboy, and when the profession collapsed he strove mightily to place as many as he could in jobs on the railways. "He had", said a man who had once driven one of Chaplin's coaches, "a very good knowledge of the animals he governed as well as the bipeds with whom he was associated. . . . With the employment of an oratory he could at all times most powerfully use, though it was not adapted to the atmosphere of St Stephen's, he added an intellect superior to most of his class in shrewdness and tact, and with this a soft, oily expression that procured for him the *sobriquet* of 'Bite 'em sly' ''. At his death (1859), he was worth nearly half a million pounds, though a large part of it had probably been accumulated during his connection with the railways.

Chaplin had a country estate near Basingstoke where, one Sunday, he attended church with a friend who was staying at the house. The sermon was about Solomon, and as they were walking home after the service, Chaplin remarked to his friend, "That Solomon was a clever fellow. I should not like to have bought a horse from him without a written warrant".

Though none operated on so big a scale as Chaplin, Sherman and Horne, there were a number of other well-known characters among London coaching proprietors. At the Bull in Aldgate, Mrs Nelson and her sons carried on the business that her husband had developed, horsing many of the East Anglian coaches. One of her sons became proprietor of the Bell Savage, on Ludgate Hill, which at its peak stabled some four hundred horses. The previous landlord of the Bell Savage, Robert Gray, moved to the Bolt-in-Tun, Fleet Street, from which several coaches ran to the south and west. Gray also horsed two of the London mails, in partnership with the elder Horne. From the Blossoms Inn, Cheapside, ran a fast night coach to Manchester called *Peveril of the Peak.* Joseph Hearn at the King's Arms, Snow Hill, ran a fast coach to Birmingham via Warwick, and Robert Fagg at the Bell and Crown, Holborn, horsed the Louth mail in partnership with Mrs Mountain of the Saracen's Head. There were some substantial coachmasters in the provinces too, like Mr Brotherton of Liverpool, Mr Piper of Edinburgh, or Mr Pickwick of the White Hart, Bath, who is mentioned in Dickens's novel about another Pickwick.

These were all substantial business people who, when the railways put an end to coaching, were able to maintain themselves by other means, the wisest of them, like Chaplin and Horne, acting on the principle that if you can't beat them, join them. In the brief golden age of coaching these people were, in the words of Stanley Harris, "a most important branch of the community . . . and large contributors to the National Exchequer in the shape of payment of heavy duties imposed in various ways on these businesses, independently of similar taxes levied upon them in their capacity of innkeepers".

TEN

Expeditious Travelling

What most impressed contemporaries in the golden age of
coaching was the sheer speed at which coaches travelled. For
hundreds of years man had been able to travel as fast as a horse
could run – but only for short distances and on suitable surfaces.
On the new roads, coaches travelled the length of the country at
a speed that would have seemed unthinkable two or three
generations earlier. Diaries and letters of the period are full of
remarks about the rapidity of journeys by coach. People never
ceased to marvel that they could travel from, say, Shrewsbury to
London in a single day – until the railways came.

We have become accustomed to a far more remarkable
acceleration in the speed of public transport, and travel from
London to New York in seven hours unmoved by the experience.
The admiration and astonishment that greeted the performance
of the coach is bound to seem quaint. Yet that performance really
was extraordinary – and not only by comparison with earlier
times. Judged by time schedules alone, it can be argued that
coaching represented as great an improvement in public transport
as the railways. On the chief routes of the country, the minimum
journey time was reduced up to ten or even twenty
times between the early eighteenth century and the early
nineteenth, a reduction comparable with that achieved by the
railways during the hundred years following.

"The art of travelling has undergone great alterations in the
course of the last thirty years", wrote a stage-coach passenger in
1827, and he added, "these are not altogether improvements".

"We don't travel half so comfortably now as we used to do", lamented a Brighton coachman in 1831. "It is all hurry and bustle nowadays, Sir – no time even for a pipe and glass of grog". Speed had become an obsession with many coach proprietors, and everything was sacrificed to the schedule. Stops were cut down to as few as possible, and the interval allowed for a meal was seldom more than twenty-five minutes. Coaches ran through the night with the passengers dozing fitfully on each other's shoulders, waking every forty or fifty minutes when motion ceased while the horses were changed. Obviously, there was a public demand for speed, and presumably the majority of travellers were willing to endure the concomitant discomforts for the sake of reaching their destination as quickly as possible. But many preferred to travel more easily on a slow coach, taking a proper night's rest at an inn on the way. "No more night-travelling", wrote Charles Lamb after a journey in 1810. "My head is sore . . . with that deduction of my natural rest which I suffered coming down."

"One great mistake amongst people who do not see much of the road", wrote a correspondent of the *New Sporting Magazine* in 1831, "is to imagine, when they hear of a fast coach, that there must be galloping and racing. These two sins, indefensible at all times, are never committed on a regular concern." "Never" is overstating the case, yet high average speed was achieved not by a mad gallop but by a steady trot. The difference in speed between a gallop and trot is not, in fact, so large as it looks, but in any case horses cannot be asked to gallop for ten miles or more even on the kindest surface. There were certain well-known spots on the chief roads where it was advisable to 'spring' (i.e. gallop) the horses, mainly on stretches just before hills, to give the team a good start up the slope. An experienced coachman on hilly ground could judge where to hold his team back on a downward slope and when to give them their heads so that they would have a running start on the hill ahead without upsetting the coach at the bottom of the slope they were descending. This could not be done, of course, if there were a drag on the wheels, another reason why coachmen tended, perilously, to ignore that precaution.

On some of the main roads there were certain exceptionally good stretches, broad and level for several miles, where the horses might be sprung without undue risk if time had to be made up or an opposition coach outdistanced. On the Holyhead road there was a stage south of Coventry where five miles could be covered in less than twenty minutes. The west-bound coaches out of London had six miles of 'galloping ground' beyond Hounslow, known as "the hospital ground" according to Nimrod, where all the bad horses were put to work "because *here* they had nothing to do but gallop". One of the best stretches for galloping, where rival coaches were often tempted to race each other, lay farther west on the Exeter road, west of Blackwater at Hartford Bridge Flat, "a very dreary and dismal tract of country", according to W. Outram Tristram, but known as "the best five miles for a coach in all England". Experienced coachmen who knew other places on the road where they might gain a minute or two by galloping their team without losing control of them could sometimes be tempted into a short sprint if none of the passengers objected — and sometimes when they did. ("What are your lives and limbs to me?" one galloping coachman replied to a nervously complaining passenger. "I am behind my time.")

Considering all the inevitable delays during a journey of 100 miles or more — the frequent changing of horses, the steep hills or sharp turns that enforced a walking pace, the minor hold-ups of one kind or another that occur on any journey — the long-distance coaches maintained remarkably high average speeds. Many of the most famous coaches regularly completed their journeys at an average speed, including stops, of over ten miles an hour. The Shrewsbury *Wonder* was scheduled to depart from the Bull and Mouth at 6.30 in the morning and from the Peacock, Islington (where Tom Brown caught the coach for Rugby), fifteen minutes later. It arrived at Shrewsbury at 10.30 p.m., 14 hours 45 minutes after leaving London, covering the 158 miles at an average speed of 10.7 miles an hour. Time allowed for halts on the journey was eighty minutes, so the average travelling speed was 11.8 miles an hour. Before it was taken off, the *Wonder* improved even on this.

Another of Sherman's fast day-coaches, the Manchester *Telegraph*, had a longer journey — 186 miles. It left one and a half hours earlier than the *Wonder* and arrived at Manchester at 11.30 p.m., an average speed, including stops, of 10.2 miles an hour. It was usually said that a speed of 11 miles an hour or more could not be maintained without galloping. If true, the *Wonder* and the Manchester *Telegraph* must have galloped on some stages in order to keep to their times, and the *Independent Tally-Ho*, which is said to have covered the 109 miles from London to Birmingham in $7\frac{1}{2}$ hours – an average speed of 14.5 miles an hour – certainly did so. This was an exceptional time, however, which was recorded in 1830 on May day, when it was the custom all over the country for coaches to go flat out. Another famous Birmingham coach, the *Tantivy*, took twelve hours, but it went by the longer route through Oxford and Stratford-on-Avon and averaged just under 10.5 miles an hour, including stops. The average speed of all the daily coaches between London and Bristol was just under 10 miles an hour.

By about 1830, travel times on major routes had, in general, been reduced to about one quarter of what they were in the middle of the eighteenth century and journey times (including stops) by much more. An old man going to Shrewsbury on the *Wonder* might just have remembered when the journey took four days. What excitement there had been when in 1764 'Fowler's Shrewsbury Stage-coach' managed to cut the journey time in half though, admittedly, this coach was a 'butterfly' (running in the summer months only). The introduction of the mails reduced the time to twenty-four hours and by 1822, not long before the *Wonder* was introduced, it was down to eighteen hours. The *Wonder* lopped off over three hours on its first running and, by 1835, had improved its own time by another two hours.

To travel from Shrewsbury or Birmingham or, more remarkably, from Manchester to London in a single day would have seemed fantastic less than a hundred years earlier. For many people, not just those who travelled by coach, the new rapidity of travel brought many changes. It was now feasible, though not, perhaps, very desirable, for a businessman to spend half the week in London and half in Birmingham. Orders could be given in London on a Monday for something to be done in almost any part of the kingdom, and before Friday the man who gave the orders would have news of how they were carried out. This was Expeditious Travelling! No wonder, as the coach rolled through the countryside, farm workers straightened their stiff backs to watch it pass and in every settlement young and old hurried to the windows when they heard the sound of the coaching horn. Equally impressive were the times recorded by the long-distance coaches. The Devonport mail, known as the *Quicksilver*, was probably the most reliable of these. It left London along with all the night mails at 8 p.m., crossed Salisbury Plain at dead of night, and arrived at Exeter soon after midday. It stopped there ten minutes and was away again, reaching Devonport soon after 5 p.m. In 1837, when these times were kept, it then crossed by the ferry where Brunel was to build the Saltash bridge and proceeded on to Falmouth (the port for the West Indies mail packets), which it reached one hour after midnight. Between London and Devonport, the average speed was just over ten miles an hour, very good going for a journey of 215 miles and including stops for changing the mail bags as well as changing the horses. The time for the whole journey to Falmouth was 29 hours 5 minutes, the total distance 271 miles; average speed including stops, ferry ride, etc., 9.3 miles an hour.

The Holyhead road via Shrewsbury was, thanks to Telford, one of the best in the country, and many of the fastest coaches used it. A friend of Nimrod remarked on a speedy journey he had undertaken on this route in about 1830:

"I was out hunting last season, on a Monday, near Brighton, and dined with my father in Merrion Square, Dublin, at six o'clock on the following Wednesday, distance four hundred miles".

"It was done thus", says Nimrod. "He went from Brighton in an afternoon coach that set him down in London in time for the Holyhead Mail, and this mail, with the help of the steamer to cross the Channel, delivered him in Dublin at the time mentioned."

"What would the writer say now", wondered Lord William Pitt Lennox, quoting this story over forty years later, "when, by leaving London at 7.15 a.m., he may dine at the table-d'hôte at the Shelbourne Hotel, Dublin, at 7.30 p.m., with ample time to have a hot bath and change his dress before dinner is served?" And what would Lord William say now, when, by leaving London at that same time, he would arrive in his Dublin hotel in time for a late breakfast?

The journey from London to Exeter, which the *Quicksilver* Devonport mail accomplished in 16½ hours, had, almost within

living memory, taken five or six days. In the seventeenth century
it had taken two weeks. The first stage-coach between
Edinburgh and Glasgow (44 miles) had taken three days when it
was started in 1678 — if, indeed it ran, which is uncertain. The
first regular service, begun in 1749, took two days, reduced to a
day and a half some ten years later. In 1831, two rival stage-
coaches left Glasgow at 6 a.m. and set down their passengers in
Princes Street at 9.42. It took scarcely longer to travel from
Edinburgh to London by the mail than it had taken to go from
Edinburgh to Glasgow fifty years earlier (the time allowed from
London to Edinburgh in a timebill of 1837 was 42 hours 23
minutes).

Besides travelling very fast the mails and the crack day-coaches
were also remarkably punctual. Old waybills show that the time
on each stage was calculated almost to the second, and several old
coaching writers insist that people used to set their watches by
the passing of the coach. No one then, of course, could turn on
the radio or telephone the 'speaking clock', and people were altogether less precise about time than they have since become. Still,
the regularity of coaches had improved astonishingly since
the days when a passenger on the Dover road inquired of the
coachman what time he arrived in London and received the
answer that "the proper hour was six o'clock, but he had been
every hour of the four-and-twenty after it".

No less striking than improved speed and punctuality was the
increase in services during the period 1815–1835. It was estimated
that in 1830 some 300 coaches daily passed through the tollgate at
Hyde Park Corner; so heavy was the traffic that the gates were
kept permanently open. The arrivals and departures from a big
coaching inn at a place like Hounslow must have been as
disturbing to the local people as the arrivals and departures of jet
airliners are to the present inhabitants of that borough, and
almost as frequent.

An article in the press in 1824 estimated that some 1,500
coaches left London every day. There were forty coaches daily to
Brighton and more than forty to Birmingham, nearly twenty to
Chester and nearly sixty to Liverpool, which had no London
coach before 1769. Among others, eighteen went daily to York,
twelve to Hull and twelve to Preston. For some places,
moreover, these figures were on the low side: the number of

daily Brighton coaches for instance was probably more than forty in 1824. Other cities were no less busy. William Tuckwell remembered entering Oxford on the Henley road in the reign of William IV, when "along the road, or into Oxford by the St Giles's entrance . . . sped stage-coaches all day long — *Tantivy, Defiance, Rival, Regulator, Mazeppa, Telegraph, Rocket,* 'a fast coach, which performed the journey from Oxford to Birmingham in seven hours', *Dart, Magnet, Blenheim,* and some thirty more; heaped high with ponderous luggage and with cloaked passengers". In Cupar, Fife, 783 stage-coach passengers passed through the town in one week in 1827; a generation earlier, that road supported but one coach north and one south per week.

When the Great Western Railway, from London to Bristol, was being contemplated in 1832, twenty-two stage-coaches were running daily up and down between the two cities, plus four mails (two up, two down). According to the railway company's figures, the coaches on this ground were fairly full; nine was said to be the average number of stage-coach passengers, five of the mails.

Although these numbers represent a huge advance on the number of coach passengers travelling half a century earlier, the total is still small compared with the number carried by the railways half a century later. Although coaches were used by all classes of the population except the very poorest, they were not used *often* — not because they were uncomfortable or slow but because they were expensive. Although fares were considearbly reduced in the 1820s and 1830s, travel was still a costly business and most people travelled only when they had to.

In 1812, Colonel Hawker travelled from London to Glasgow with his man-servant. He took the mail, the fastest but most expensive, and wisely broke his journey three times to spend the night in a bed, which may have resulted in a slight increase in the total fares. The cost for himself was £10 8s. His servant travelled outside, and cost the Colonel another £6 5s. On top of that, tips amounted to £2 17s, making a grand total, excluding food and lodging, of £19 10s.

The actual fare was high enough, but unavoidable incidental expenses raised the cost twenty or thirty per cent. In 1830 the fare from London to Newcastle, outside, was £3 10s but, according to C.G. Harper's reckoning, tips to guards and coachmen would have cost 14s and meals (supper, a late snack, breakfast, dinner and tea) about the same, raising the total for the journey to nearly £5. An inside seat, which required a higher rate of tipping, would have cost about £8, considerably more than the 2nd-class rail fare in 1974.

Competition and, later, the threat of the railways combined to cause sharp reductions in fares. In 1834 it was possible to travel from London to Birmingham for £1 inside, half as much outside, and to Liverpool for £2 inside, £1 outside. A few years earlier, these journeys would have cost more than twice as much. At the peak of the competition on the Brighton road in about 1827, passengers were offered a free lunch, with wine, and a refund of the fare (five shillings outside) if the coach failed to keep time. This particular gimmick, a daring one in the circumstances, was first employed on the Brighton road as early as 1806, when the scheduled time was eight hours (ultimately reduced to five) and the fare more than double.

Among the busiest roads from London were the Brighton road, the Bath and Bristol road, the Exeter road, the Birmingham, Shrewsbury and Holyhead road, the Oxford and Birmingham road, the York road and the Portsmouth road; but there was plenty of coaching activity on other roads that did not lead to London. From Brighton in 1822, for instance, besides the coaches that left for London every few minutes during the day, there were two to Portsmouth, two to Southampton, six to Lewes, two to Hastings, eight to Worthing, and one each to Maidstone, Oxford and Windsor. A few years later, services were added for Chichester, Bognor and other places. At busy times of the day, Castle Square was jammed almost solid.

The son of a coachman who drove the *Oxonian* on the Oxford-Southampton road for thirty-six years, left a record of that journey as it was in about 1830.

The coach left the Angel in Oxford at 8 a.m., six days a week, called at the Mitre booking office and left by St Aldate's for the south. The coachman was a jolly fellow, always telling amusing stories and endeavouring to keep his passengers in a good mood. Between Oxford and Abingdon there was a steep hill, where the skid had to be put on before the coach could descend. Going uphill, the coachman would ask his passengers, in his sweetest tones, if they would be so kind as to assist the horses by walking up the hill. On the first stage alone there were two hills where the passengers were asked to walk; but this stage – nineteen miles – was a very long one even for a cross-country road. After changing horses at the Swann Inn, Ilsey, there was another long climb; a difficult piece of ground this, especially when the great sheep fair was being held. The next change, nine miles farther, was at the Pelican, Newbury, an inn well-known to all travellers on that road (one of whom suggested it was called 'the Pelican' because of it enormous bill!). The half-way point, near enough, was reached at the Chequers, where the coachman inquired of his passengers if they would care to take a glass of pure malt and hops brewed by the landlord? (Modern beer-drinkers, accustomed to the same characterless brew from one end of the country to the other, may here breathe a regretful sigh.)

The passengers soon had reason to be thankful for this refreshing pause as, shortly afterwards, they were again politely asked to walk a little way while the horses laboured up Beacon Hill. Then on to Whitchurch, thirteen miles, where at the White Hart there were connections with coaches for the west, and up and over the downs for another thirteen miles to Winchester and the Black Swan. Here the horses were changed for the last time before the twelve-mile run through the village of Otterbourne, to Southampton, driving for the last few miles on a good road through beautiful parkland with elm-lined drives, and pulling up at the Coach and Horses punctually at three o'clock in the afternoon. Sixty-six miles in seven hours – a very fair speed for hilly ground, and much faster than when this coachman had first driven it, some thirty years before. The *Oxonian* then had left the Angel at five in the morning and arrived at five in the afternoon.

Some coaches were associated with special events, such as race-meetings at Epsom or Newmarket, or with a particular class of passenger, such as the undergraduates who patronized certain Oxford and Cambridge coaches or the schoolboys bound for home and holidays who shared a Christmas coach with Washington Irving. A coach that was remembered nostalgically by Old Etonians who lived in the north-west was the old *Rocket* – in spite of its name a slow night coach – which ran from London via Slough and Oxford to Birmingham and Shrewsbury. At the end of term, pupils heading for those parts were allowed to leave the night before breaking-up in order to catch the *Rocket* at Slough at 7 p.m. On these thrice-yearly occasions, the coach arrived empty at Slough, presumably by previous arrangement with the college. It can easily be imagined that no coach ever had a noisier or happier load, for the boys, as Edward Corbett recalled, "right well filled it, inside and out, though the latter was the most coveted position, as being thought more manly". The conscientious Corbett parents booked an inside seat for their young son at Christmas, but he made a straight exchange with some tenderer sprig booked on the outside.

The *Rocket* stopped for supper at Oxford where, when the Eton boys were expected, an extra-large meal was provided, then proceeded on to Birmingham, arriving at 8 a.m. No one got much sleep, but "we did know what cold feet were before arriving at Birmingham". The coach was half-smothered with luggage, no inch of space remaining unoccupied, with odd articles tied precariously to the lamp brackets and other parcels attached to the rear axle below the coach. Among the latter, on one occasion when Edward Corbett was among the homeward-bound Etonians, was a basket of fish, to be delivered at some place along the road. It was a frosty night, the road was hard, and when the coachman went to retrieve the basket, he found the bottom had been knocked out and the cod and oysters distributed somewhere back along the road.

Between Birmingham and Shrewsbury the *Rocket* was driven by an old coachman named Rook, who had not been infected with the new passion for strict timekeeping. His passengers being highly appreciative of any entertainment the passing world might provide, he often stopped along the road, chiefly to relieve the dryness in his throat, but sometimes for leisurely observation of interesting incidents. Some men baiting a bull on a piece of open ground in the village of Bilston provided the cause for one such delay. It was said of old Rook that he would sometimes stop to give a lift to a friend, but the friend, if he were in a hurry, would politely decline.

Perhaps a coach-load of upper-class youths, impregnated with confidence in their superiority by birth, was not the coachman's idea of perfection. They were useful for waking a sleepy tollkeeper, which they did by shouting "Fire!" (they found that "Murder" had no effect), but the boisterous behaviour of the young passengers must have added to the normal hazards of a journey. Once, when the young Corbett and some fellow pupils travelled to London by postchaise, they amused themselves by hurling pennies to break the shop windows all the way from Slough to Brentford. The temptation to hurl missiles from – or at – a moving vehicle first became a serious menace with the stage-coach, although the missiles were usually less damaging than copper coins. The pea-shooter was the normal weapon of irresponsible young persons (and some not so young) seeking entertainment from the rear seats of a stage-coach. In remote places, roadside piles of stones for repairing the surface provided ammunition for ignorant country youths. Passengers passing through little settlements in Sutherland and Caithness were sometimes forced to lie on the floor to escape flying glass. A coachman from Wick lost an eye; two horses, standing unattended, were stoned to death.

For every person who wished to travel from one town to another by the stage-coach, there were many who required transport for a much shorter distance. Scheduled urban passenger transport hardly existed anywhere before the nineteenth century, largely because cities were so small that there was no need for it. Except in London, a short walk would take you from one side of the town to the other.

Hackney carriages (the words mean simply carriages for hire) were fairly numerous in London in the reign of James I, and throughout the seventeenth century there were complaints about their proliferating numbers. Under the Commonwealth they were limited to 300 in the cities of London and Westminster and permitted to carry fares within a radius of six miles. In 1663 the licensed number was increased to 400; in 1715 it was doubled, and in 1768 raised to 1,000. That remained the legal total until 1832, when it was increased to 1200; but it is doubtful that these numbers accurately record the actual number of vehicles on the streets. The hackney business was always a rough, free-and-easy trade; hackneymen and sedan chairmen tended to be individualists, inclined to resort to their fists to sort out arguments over fares and frequently engaged in a running battle with rivals such as watermen and stage-coachmen, as well as the authorities. Periods of strict regulation and control of hackney carriages and sedan chairs alternated with periods of near-anarchy, apparently tolerated by government. W.T. Jackman quotes figures in the Treasury Papers showing receipts from licenses for sedan chairs: in the year 1742, receipts for 400 licenses were recorded without comment, although the official maximum allowed was 200.

Scheduled public services came much later. The rise of the omnibus, basically a light van holding twenty or more people and drawn by a pair of horses, is usually dated from 1829 when George Shillibeer, an interesting character who at other times pursued different trades, including those of smuggler and undertaker, put on the London Streets two such vehicles called the *Omnibus* and the *Shillibeer* (oddly enough, it was the latter name that was more often used to describe the type in the early years). However, there were omnibuses to be seen in London much earlier, certainly before the end of the eighteenth century. Unlike the stage-coach, the omnibus did not suffer by the advent of railways; in fact, business increased. The development of the omnibus was continuous, leading eventually to the double-decker of today, fabled in song and story.

Between the mail- and stage-coach on the one hand and the hackney carriage and omnibus on the other, came the 'short-stage'. The short-stage was simple a stage-coach that ran a short distance; for instance, between the city centre and the suburbs. It was usually drawn by two horses rather than four and, being a vehicle more mundane and easier to drive than the stage-coach, it scarcely figures in the literature of coaching: Hazlitt felt nothing but contempt for the Putney and Brentford stages that drew up in Piccadilly after the dashing mails had departed. Nevertheless, the short-stage provided an important service. It has been estimated that in the 1820s nearly 2000 journeys were performed daily between London and the suburbs, each coach managing an average of three or four journeys a day. From the city to Uxbridge, seven short-stages performed the eighteen-mile journey twice (in each direction) every day, taking three hours one way. Fashionable Richmond, only one-and-a-half hours from town, had fourteen coaches, each rattling over Kew Bridge five or six times daily.

The big stage-coach proprietors had nothing to do with these short-stages, which they regarded as tiresome and vulgar obstacles to the progress of grander vehicles. They set out from a number of small, obscure inns (most of them long vanished) like the Goose and Gridiron in St Paul's Churchyard, and stopped at numerous other places along the route, or at randon when hailed by a passenger. Some very peculiar vehicles were to be found among them – old private carriages too dilapidated for their original owners, stage-coaches retired from business, and the occasional brainchild of some eccentric amateur coachbuilder, bought cheaply through lack of demand. The business was run in a – to put it politely – informal way. Regulations concerning the number of passengers permitted were liberally interpreted, and arguments about fares or luggage kept everyone entertained. The often-quoted account by Louis Simond of a journey by short-stage from Richmond in 1810 is, if a little colourful, probably not too unfair.

> . . . The stage-coach was crammed inside and *hérisse* outside with pasengers of all sexes, ages and conditions. We stopped more than twenty times on the road – the debates about the fare of the way-passengers – the settling themselves – the getting up, and the getting down, and damsels showing their legs in the operation, and tearing and muddying their petticoats – complaining and swearing – took an immense time. I never saw anything so ill managed. In about two hours we reached Hyde Park Corner. . . .

It does not really sound much different from the same journey today when performed by bus in the rush hour.

ELEVEN

Grim Predicaments

A coach and four, whatever its attractions, was far from the most comfortable or the safest means of travel ever invented. "Eight miles an hour, for twenty or five-and-twenty hours, a tight mail-coach, a hard seat, a gouty tendency, a perpetual change of coachmen grumbling because you did not fee them enough, a fellow-passenger partial to spirits-and-water – who has not borne these evils in the jolly old times"? asked Thackeray, "and how could people travel under such difficulties?"

Outside passengers suffered special discomforts. De Quincey and other enthusiasts convey the exhilaration of riding outside on a fast coach, but who could enjoy perching on top of a rumbling box in the depth of winter, with snow or rain blowing into his face? The "glory of motion" was not evident when the coach was proceeding at a cautious walk through a thick November fog. The coachman did not keep his eager clients amused with anecdotes of the road while he was trying to manoeuvre his coach along an icy road in darkness and a freezing gale. Splashed by puddles, soaked by rain, jolted by ruts, blown by winds, and chilled by frosts, the outside passenger did not have an easy time. Besides the panegyric of De Quincey must be placed the dire report of an equally amusing but less contented traveller, the German pastor Karl Philipp Moritz, who travelled in England in 1782.

In those days the mail-coach had not yet appeared, and coaches in general were far more primitive than they were when De Quincey travelled with the news of Talavera. That curious posterior appendage, the basket, was found on most stage-coaches, including that on which Moritz journeyed from Leicester to Northampton. "I observe", he wrote, "that they have here a curious way of riding, not in, but upon, a stage-coach. Persons to whom it is not convenient to pay a full price, instead of the inside, sit on the top of the coach, without any seats or even a rail". He had not much money, and decided to try this station himself. It was a journey, he said, that he would remember as long as he lived.

To begin with, he found that the outside passengers were not able to get on board in the innyard without the risk of losing their heads against the low arch leading to the street. They had to wait until the coach had passed out of the yard and scramble up to the roof on a ladder in the street. "The getting up alone was at the risk of one's life, and when I was up I was obliged to sit just at the corner of the coach, with nothing to hold on by but a sort of little handle fastened on the side. I sat nearest the wheel, and the moment that we set off I fancied I saw certain death before me." The coach rattled over the cobbles with what seemed extraordinary speed, while Moritz and three others on the roof hung on grimly, bouncing into the air at every jolt. It seemed inevitable that before long they would be hurled from their precarious perch, and Moritz, desperately seeking safety, crawled over the roof and dropped into the basket behind. He felt intense relief at being saved from imminent destruction, but soon found that his new situation was no improvement.

As long as we went on slowly up the hill, it was easy and pleasant enough; and then I was just on the point of falling asleep, having had no rest the night before, when on a sudden the coach proceeded at a rapid rate downhill. Then all the boxes, iron-nailed and copper-fastened, began, as it were, to dance around me; everything in the basket appeared to be alive, and every moment I received such violent blows that I thought my last hour had come. . . . I was obliged to suffer horrible torture for nearly an hour, which seemed to me an eternity. At last we came to another hill, when, quite shaken to pieces, bleeding and sore, I ruefully crept back to the top of the coach to my former seat . . . and I now write this as a warning to all strangers who are inclined to ride in English stage-coaches and take an outside seat, or, worse still, horror of horrors, a seat in the basket.

For the remainder of his journey to London, Moritz booked an inside seat. He was no longer in fear of being hurled into the road or pounded to a pulp, but he was still far from happy.

> The journey . . . I can scarcely call a ride, for it was a perpetual motion, or endless jolt from one place to another, in a close wooden box, over what appeared to be a heap of unhewn stones and trunks of trees scattered by a hurricane. To make my unhappiness complete, I had three travelling companions, all farmers, who slept so soundly that even the hearty knocks with which they hammered their heads against each other and against mine did not awaken them. Their faces, bloated and discoloured by ale and brandy and the knocks aforesaid, looked, as they lay before me, like so many lumps of dead flesh. I looked, and certainly felt, like a crazy fool when we arrived at London. . . .

Moritz did not enjoy his English travels. He found that a foreigner — worse, a poor foreigner — was slightingly treated by the landlords, servants and coachmen that he encountered. It is sometimes supposed that snobbery and class-consciousness were largely the inventions of the Victorians, and in a certain sense that may be true. But anyone who has read an eighteenth-century novel must be aware of the obsession with social status that existed long before the 'public-school system' became institutionalized. Social gradations may have been less rigid, but they were jealously guarded all the same, and they assumed extra emphasis on the road where, divorced from their normal environment, people feared that their social standing might be underrated, or seized the opportunity to assume a status superior to their true one — like the lady picked up by the York coach in *Nicholas Nickleby* who "loudly lamented, for the behoof of the outsides, the non-arrival of her own carriage which was to have taken her on, and made the guard solemnly promise to stop every green chariot he saw coming". Needless to say, no such conveyance materialized. (Among the passengers in a coach, says Thackeray, there was always a "prim lady, who declare[s] upon her sacred honour she [has] never travelled in a public carriage before".)

On the stage-coaches of the eighteenth century, there was none of that horsey pretentiousness that resulted from aristocratic patronage in later times; knights and baronets were not yet to be seen on the boxes of public coaches, nor indeed seated inside. But those who did take inside seats on the coach regarded themselves as a cut above those who rode outside; the difference was certainly as great as that between first class and third, if not between state-room and steerage, and the word 'outsider' has stuck in the language as a term of snobbish distaste. De Quincey described the absurdities of this convention in his essay on the mail-coach.

> Up to this time, say 1804, or 1805 (the year of Trafalgar), it had been the fixed assumption of the four inside people . . . that they, the illustrious quarternion, constituted a porcelain variety of the human race, whose dignity would have been compromised by exchanging one word of civility with the three miserable delftware outsides. . . . What word, then, could express the horror, and the sense of treason, in that case, which *had* happened, when all three outsides (the trinity of Pariahs) made a vain attempt to sit down at the same breakfast-table or dinner-table with the consecrated four? I myself witnessed such an attempt; and on that occasion a benevolent old gentleman endeavoured to soothe his three holy associates, by suggesting that, if the outsides were indicted for this criminal attempt at the next assizes, the court would regard it as a case of lunacy, or *delirium tremens*, rather than of treason. . . . The course taken with the infatuated outsiders . . . was that the waiter, beckoning them away from the privileged *salle-à-manger*, sang out, "This way, my good men", and then enticed these good men away to the kitchen.

At the time De Quincey was describing, the class division between inside and outside was already passing away, largely because young men of fairly impeccable background like De Quincey and his friends found the outside of the coach preferable to the inside, regardless of cost. They decided, says De Quincey, "that the roof of the coach, which by some weak men had been called the attics, and by some the garrets, was in reality the drawing room; in which drawing room the box was the chief ottoman or sofa; whilst it appeared that the *inside*, which had been traditionally regarded as the only room tenantable by gentlemen, was, in fact, the coal-cellar in disguise".

Conditions had changed in the twenty or thirty years since Moritz had been bounced and banged to Northampton. The horrid basket had disappeared, seats and rails were installed on the roof, better springs and better roads had made travelling outside less dangerous and less uncomfortable.

Although Moritz, like De Quincey in his very different style, liked to exaggerate, his fear of being hurled to destruction from the top of the coach was not groundless. Cyril Noall relates an incident in Cornwall in the winter of 1836, which might have ended in a nasty accident.

A mail-coach was crossing Dartmoor several miles west of Okehampton when the solitary passenger, seated inside, felt a sudden, severe jolt. The horses broke into a gallop and, assuming that the coachman was trying to make up time, the passenger hung on grimly as the coach thundered through the snow. Eventually it came to a stop at a tollgate and, puzzled by the delay, the passenger put his head out of the window to see what was going on. Only then did he discover that he was alone on the coach. The jolt, caused by a heap of stones, had toppled both driver and guard from their seats, and the horses had taken off by themselves. The missing crew appeared some time later, the coachman nursing a broken arm but otherwise without serious injury.

A rather similar incident in the same region of the country occurred some years later, when the Bath-Devonport mail was left unattended outside an inn. With no one to hold them, the horses declined to wait for the coachman and guard to finish their drinks and set off at their usual smart trot towards Plymouth, to the consternation of Mrs Cox, a large Devonport fishwife who was the only outside passenger. Gesturing frantically to passers-by, Mrs Cox yet had the sense not to scream, for fear of startling the horses, and the inside passengers, supposing the coachman was in his place, knew nothing of their precarious situation. The horses were an experienced team; they trotted steadily for seven miles, negotiating with aplomb all obstacles on their route, which included a bridge and a tollgate as well as oncoming traffic, and finally drew to a halt outside the King's Arms, dead on schedule.

Not all horses were so well behaved. A nasty accident occurred in Ewell in April, 1826, when the boy left in charge of the horses unthinkingly cracked the whip, which the coachman had left on the box. The horses bolted down the street, failed to negotiate a bend, and crashed into a fence. All the outside passengers were thrown off, and one of them died of her injuries – "in the greatest agony", so the newspaper reported.

Leaving the horses unattended was a mistake all too easy to make, and it resulted in many runaway coaches. An old coachman told Lord Algernon St Maur that he once met two coaches in one night without any coachman, and managed to stop them both without accident.

Nimrod has some advice for outside passengers on a runaway coach: "Never think of quitting a coach by jumping *from the fore part of her*". He relates the experience of a friend of his caught in this predicament when the reins broke and the coachman, whose box he was sharing, was thrown off. The horses broke into a gallop and a fat man on the roof, ignoring the advice of Nimrod's friend, leaped off and was killed. "My friend kept his seat for more than a mile [and] watched the opportunity of the coach running near to a high foot-path, to jump upon it, and was not at all hurt." But Nimrod adds a rider: "Now had I been in my friend's situation, I should have got over the roof into the guard's seat, and descended thence to the ground".

Sometimes, horses bolted with the coachman still in place, especially if he were an inexperienced driver. The unfortunate accident that befell the Brighton *Quicksilver* (named, like a number of others, after the famous Devonport mail) on 24th July 1833, may have been due to this cause, as it was being driven at the time not by the regular coachman but by the young son of the proprietor. Something startled the team into bolting and, as they swerved around a cart in their path, they 'floored' the coach. Several of the passengers were badly injured, though none was killed. The proprietors of the *Quicksilver* feared that this well-publicised accident would be bad for business, and accordingly changed the name of the coach to *Criterion*. But the superstition among sailors that it is unlucky to change the name of a ship perhaps had some influence among coaches too, for the career of the newly named *Criterion* was unlucky. Less than a year after the accident in Brighton, the coachman of the *Criterion* was charged with running into and damaging a private carriage in the same town. He had failed to stop and thus could not be identified, though it would seem that identification of the coach ought to have been enough to identify the coachman, a well-known local figure, as well.

Less than three months later, the *Criterion* was involved in a far worse accident. Near London Bridge, it side-swiped a dray; but no harm appeared to have been done and it proceeded on its way. A little farther on, a startled horse ran right in front of the coach, and the coachman did well to halt his team so quickly that a collision was avoided. But these two incidents had been enough to crack the pole which, when the coach started off again, broke in two and fell against the hind legs of the wheelers. The startled horses bolted and, before they could be checked, overturned the coach, killing one of the passengers (who, incidentally, was at the time following Nimrod's advice by crawling over the roof towards the rear).

The proprietors of the *Quicksilver/Criterion* were perhaps unduly sensitive in attempting to obliterate the memory of an accident by changing the coach's name. Even so famous a coach as the *Comet*, one of the classiest on the Brighton road between 1820 and 1840, suffered several overturns, with at least one fatality, in its otherwise splendid career.

Many things could go wrong on a coach journey. The traces might snap and the horses bolt, a wheel might break and the coach capsize, the horses might be sick, the coachman drunk, the coach overloaded, the road flooded – there was no end to the list of possible disasters to worry the nervous traveller. The Louth mail was upset when the leaders were startled by a donkey rolling in the dust, and the Exeter mail was once attacked by a lioness, an eventuality which the most comprehensive precautions could scarcely have prevented (the lioness had escaped from a travelling menagerie). J.B. Scott of Bungay recorded a mishap at Rochester on the way home from France in 1814, when the Dover coach was "delayed two hours by the wheel catching fire . . .", the result, unusual but not unique, of an overheated axle.

But the fact was that the great majority of accidents on the road, then as now, were caused partly or wholly by human error or neglect. "I am quite prepared to show", said Nimrod, "that ninety out of a hundred [accidents] are the effect of carelessness." Traces do not break if the harness is regularly inspected and replaced when worn. Wheels do not hit kerb stones if the driver is paying attention to his work.

The commonest cause of serious injury was an overturn. In the eighteenth century, coaches were extremely high off the ground, and although later models were much lower, they were still somewhat top-heavy. This drawback was commonly recognized, and a multitude of schemes were aired for overcoming it. The problem was aggravated by carrying passengers and luggage on the roof. The wise coachman made sure before starting that his load was distributed as evenly as possible and that heavy boxes were firmly fixed in position. Mr Weller sen. did not neglect this precaution. "Now it's time I was up at the office to get my vay-bill, and see the coach loaded; for coaches, Sammy, is like guns – they requires to be loaded with wery great care, afore they go off".

A badly loaded coach tended to sway, and a swaying coach was unstable. A large stone under one wheel and over she went. A rut in the surface had the same effect, and so did too sharp a turn, which caused the wheels to lock.

Sometimes, of course, accidents happened through bad luck alone, and nobody could be blamed, though public suspicion and gossip often ensured that someone was. An anonymous traveller on the Brighton road wrote to defend the reputation of a coachman-proprietor named Pattenden, who had been losing business since his coach was upset in Ewell. The coach, wrote the correspondent, who signed himself "Justice", was doing a moderate speed when

> one of the wheel-horses fell, on which Mr Pattenden, with the intention of making him spring up again, applied the whip. This, however, failed in the effect of raising the wheel-horse, and unfortunately occasioned the two leaders, very spirited animals, to dart forward, drag the coach upon the fallen horse, and overturned it. The horse, which had but last summer cost Mr Pattenden £35, was killed on the spot, and one of the passengers was slightly hurt; Mr Pattenden himself was violently precipitated from the box, and his head thereby was so much bruised that he was for some time in great danger, but from which situation he is now happily recovered [sufficiently, could it be, to write an anonymous letter to the press?] Can any blame here attach to the unfortunate proprietor? He was driving very moderately, and was quite sober, so that he cannot be accused either of rashness or inebriety. The place where the coach was overturned was a very wide and level piece of ground, which saved him from the blame of unskilfulness. Yet . . . malicious reports have been circulated, which have so much prejudiced the public that Mr Pattenden has, in consequence, lost a great deal of that custom upon which he depends for his own support, and that of his wife and family.

It seems unlikely that this letter from "Justice" did the trick. Mr Pattenden (if it is the same man) later appears as the landlord of an inn, an inn, alas, which was sold at auction in 1827 owing to the bankruptcy of its proprietor.

Whatever the truth about Mr Pattenden's mishap, it was hard to blame the coachman for a wheel snapping off or an axletree breaking, accidents that might happen without warning; but even then, regular inspection and maintenance would have prevented many such incidents, and there were warning signs that an alert coachman might spot. Watch out, says Nimrod, that the wheels of your coach when going straight make two tracks and not four.

No one, coachman, coachbuilder or coach proprietor, could be blamed for the difficulties caused by wind and snow, frost and flood. The weather, in the winter months at least, was the coachman's worst enemy, albeit an enemy that was seldom wholly victorious. Through hailstorm, thunder and gales, the coaches kept remarkably good time. Occasionally, freak winds blew a coach over; more often, floods made roads impassable for a day or two, or frost made hills so slippery that no coach could ascend the slope. The one thing that brought the whole business to a complete stop was a heavy snowfall.

It was not the snow falling that stopped the coaches, as many coaching prints confirm, nor snow lying evenly on the ground; but when the wind blew the snow into drifts, filling the valleys where the roads ran, then for a few days all travellers stayed put and no mail was delivered. Those unlucky enough to be stranded in the country staggered through the snow to the nearest inn, where they remained until the weather improved, perhaps amusing themselves, like the travellers in Dickens's stories, by telling tales around the fire. One party, snowed up in Dunchurch on the Holyhead road, made up a shooting party, but they had only two guns among them and their bag was small. Jack Goodwin, guard on the *Beehive*, shot a hare, but that was all. That evening they joined other stranded passengers at an inn down the road for a party, and the following day the irrepressible Jack Goodwin organized a group of singers, backed by his own bugle on which he was a notable performer, and serenaded nearby farms, where they were entertained with home-made wine and meat pies.

During the winter months, the mails carried, in adddition to their other equipment, a snow shovel strapped behind the guard's seat. But a shovel was not much use in a really heavy snowstorm, like that which swept England at Christmastime, 1836. "Never before within recollection", said a writer in *The Times*, with slight exaggeration, "was the London mail stopped for a whole night at a few miles from London, and never before have we seen the intercourse between the southern shores of England and the Metropolis interrupted for two whole days". While others were sleeping off their Christmas dinner, the mail guards struggled through snow drifts ten or twenty feet deep and, in their efforts to carry the mail forward, gained new honour for their trade which, in two or three short years, was to disappear before what Edmund Vale calls "the railway-rot". According to Captain Malet, "on the 27th there were fourteen mail-coaches abandoned in the various roads but in all cases the bags were removed, the horses extricated". Prodigious efforts were made by some of the guards; one was found dead in the snow, the mail bags hung around his neck, after he had abandoned the coach for one of the horses and then, when the snow became too much for the horse, had struggled forward on foot. The Post Office Superintendent of the Mails issued a notice of acknowledgment to all mail guards: "I have hourly proofs of the great exertions made by the guards to get the mails forwarded through the snow, and almost wonders have been performed: this is most gratifying to the Postmaster-General . . .'.

Nothing else succeeded in stopping the mails in their tracks, not even a good old-fashioned London pea-souper. Fog certainly slowed them down, however, for their lamps then were useless. They inched their way along the streets at a walk, preceded by a man carrying a flaming torch.

The driver of a down mail, having passed through Hounslow on his way west one foggy night, was surprised to hear a familiar voice greeting him from the box of a faster coach as it passed him in the dimness. "Charley, what are you doing on my road?" he called. But it turned out that he had himself taken the wrong fork out of Hounslow and would soon have found himself in Staines, instead of Slough, had his friend not corrected him.

Worse than fog or even heavy snow, though usually less widespread, was heavy rain, or rather the effect of heavy rain. "Give me a collision, a broken axle and an overturn, a runaway team, a drunken coachman, snowstorms, howling tempests", said one traveller, "but Heaven preserve us from floods!"

River banks were not so carefully maintained as they are now, drainage in rural areas was almost unknown, locks, sluices and barricades were far fewer. Floods were therefore common. The Trent, for instance, was notoriously prone to overflowing, swamping the Great North Road north of Newark, where regular coachmen became accustomed to water up to the axles or even higher. One of James Pollard's paintings shows a mail-coach proceeding through water almost up to the tops of the wheels, and though a lady inside is looking apprehensive, coachman and outsiders appear unmoved. Inside passengers were not in the best situation in such circumstances. If the horses strayed from the road or fell into an unsuspected dip, it was the inside passengers who were likely to drown.

Some horrible accidents did occur in floods. In September, 1829, the Liverpool mail had to cross a bridge under a foot or two of water. The coachman was unable to see that the centre of the bridge had been washed away, and as a result the coach plunged into the stream, drowning three of the passengers and all the horses. An old man in the Reverend Francis Kilvert's parish told him how he had once travelled from Hereford to Hay on a coach that was wrecked by a flood when the horses panicked because they could not keep their noses above water (the coachman would seem to have been at fault here). The coach was swept into the river and bobbed along like a boat for some distance. There was only one inside passenger, an elderly lady who was pulled to safety through the window; the only casualties were two horses – and the coach.

Not surprisingly, a high proportion of accidents occurred when going downhill, inevitably a tricky procedure in a vehicle so ill-provided with brakes, and one calling for both skill and judgement on the part of the coachman. First, he had to decide whether to use the drag or not. This was a matter not solely decided by the nature of the slope, which the coachman would usually be familiar with, but also by the weather conditions and the load on the coach. A heavily loaded coach naturally put a greater strain on the wheelers, which were responsible for holding it in check; but a top-heavy coach was the more inclined to topple over if the wheel were fixed. Some fine judgements had to be made.

Before descending a long hill, the wise coachman pulled up his horses and, while the guard was fitting the drag, inspected his harness to make sure nothing was about to break or become unfastened. This precaution was especially important at night, when some minor fault might have developed unseen and unnoticed while the coach was on the level; but it is unlikely that coachmen often took it. (Motorists are frequently advised to check their oil and tyres at least once a week, but who does?) It caused perhaps half a minute's delay, and the coachman, under pressure to keep time, often felt he could not afford half a minute, in spite of Nimrod's belief that *"time* can be kept without sending people into *eternity"*, a destination which, he feared, might await the passengers in a coach that failed to stop at the brow of a hill.

In the golden age of coaching, coaches were safer, horses more reliable, and coachmen more skilful and more sober than they were in the eighteenth century. To judge from some accounts, coachmen in the old days were seldom entirely sober. It is not so surprising: as Stanley Harris says, "from the constant stoppages, not only at the end of different stages, but also at numerous intermediate public-houses, in the days when, comparatively speaking, no coaches were fast, the coachman was in a state of almost continuous imbibition from the commencement to the termination of his journey". Driving four-in-hand is a difficult business in the best circumstances – it is only necessary to pull on the wrong rein at a bend to cause a pile-up – and many accidents must have occured as a result of alcoholic impairment of the coachman's faculties.

In the period after about 1815, drunkenness was far less common among coachmen; those who could not hold their liquor did not hold their jobs either. Coachmen had less opportunity to get drunk because stops were short, but of course some of them managed it just the same. The nasty collision near Biggleswade between an 'up' and a 'down' mail-coach in the summer of 1837 was put down to the coachman of the up mail being so fuzzy with drink that he failed to observe the approach of the other coach. He died in the accident (which may have made it convenient to blame him), and two horses were killed, though other injuries were minor.

But while drunken coachmen were becoming less common, there arose a new hazard, which passengers in the old days had seldom been troubled with, and that was racing. Rival coaches on the same ground were determined not to be beaten to their destination. Drivers of crack stage-coaches were tempted to outpace the mails and, in spite of De Quincey, sometimes succeeded. Racing was, of course, forbidden, and probably it was less common in fact than books suggest; but a mettlesome coachman, perhaps encouraged by a 'sporting' passenger on the box-seat, could hardly be expected to maintain his steady nine-miles-an-hour trot in face of a challenge from an 'opposition' coach.

The proprietors often encouraged racing and were not dismayed by fines, telling their coachmen that if they had beaten the opposition once they could do it again.

One of the nastiest accidents caused by racing involved two mail-coaches, the Holyhead and the Chester mails, near St Albans in 1820, and resulted in charges of murder, later reduced to manslaughter, being lodged against both coachmen. The Chester mail came up to the Holyhead as they were passing through Highgate, and the Holyhead coachman, unwilling to be overtaken, cracked his whip and clapped on speed. The contest continued in an off-and-on way, with intervals of caution, until the hill just south of St Albans, when the Holyhead mail broke into a flat-out gallop down the hill. The Chester coachman saw that he could not out-pace his rival and, according to the accounts of witnesses, deliberately pulled his leaders across the Holyhead mail, causing a frightful pile-up which "in a moment converted two spick-and-span turn-outs, full of passengers more or less alive and alarmed, into a mass of struggling horseflesh, splintered wood and groaning wounded". One of the passengers was killed outright, and several others were badly injured. In passing sentence, the judge strongly condemned the behaviour of the two coachmen and pronounced it his duty to pass the severest sentence the law would allow which, however, turned out to be one year in jail.

The crash of the Chester and Holyhead mails was in several respects a freakish accident. The mails seldom raced each other, and as these two mails must have left London more or less together on the same road every evening, it is strange that they should have become involved in so intense a contest on this particular occasion. Also, it is hard to conceive of an experienced coachman who would deliberately cross in front of his rival while descending a hill at a gallop, as disastrous consequences were almost inevitable. Nevertheless, other accidents were reported apparently as a result of such a rash manoeuvre.

The man who drove the Oxford-Southampton *Oxonian* is said to have completed his journey six times a week for thirty-five years without an accident. Nimrod, who regarded himself as a pretty experienced dragsman, said that he never once had a serious accident (though by his own account he came very close to it on several occasions). Lord Algernon St Maur, an enthusiastic amateur coachman in the 1830s, "never witnessed any accident" during all the years he drove. On the other hand, both provincial and metropolitan newspapers were full of accounts of coaching accidents. As W.T. Jackman says, it is only necessary to consult the index of *The Times* under the heading "Accidents" to get "a correct idea of the great dangers from stage-coach travelling".

But is it really a correct idea? From newspaper accounts of today, historians in the future may gain a superficial impression of the great dangers of air travel. But when they compare the number of accidents with the number of flights, or the number of passenger-miles with the number of deaths, they will find that air travel was comparatively safe. Unfortunately, the data for such a quantitative study of coaching accidents are at present insufficient, but in that case too, published accounts may give a misleading impression of the frequency of accidents. The report of a coach overturned on the Brighton road naturally did not include the uninteresting news that fifty other coaches using the same road on the same day completed their journey without incident.

However, if it were possible to carry out an accurate quantitative study by collecting all published accident reports for a certain month or year and collating them with all public coach journeys, the result would almost certainly give too low a proportion of accidents, because not all accidents were reported. Minor upsets in out-of-the-way places involving unimportant people would have been overlooked, or omitted as insufficiently newsworthy. But there was more to it than that. According to the author of a book on coachbuilding published in 1810, less than ten per cent of coach accidents were reported, and the reason, he implied, was that bad news of this kind was deliberately suppressed by coach proprietors. No doubt this was an exaggeration: as designer of a new type of 'safe' coach, the author had a large axe to grind, and it is hard to believe that coach proprietors were so influential that they could keep out of print the report, for example, of a law case in which they were being sued for damages – a frequent consequence of coaching accidents. But most of the gentlemen-coachmen who published their reminiscences after the coaching age was over agree that accidents were extremely common. Lord William Pitt Lennox said he "could fill pages with accidents that have occurred to stage-coaches, in which many were killed and others most severely hurt".

Accidents were certainly common enough to make the public nervous. An 'Old Traveller' writing to the *Sporting Magazine* in October, 1822, complained, "In my younger days, when I was on the eve of setting out on a journey, my wife was in the habit of giving me her parting blessing, concluding with the words 'God bless you, my dear, I hope you will not be robbed'. But it is now changed to 'God bless you, my dear, I hope you will not get your neck broke, and that you will bring all your legs safe home again'."

In an effort to prevent accidents, particularly overturns, a number of 'patent safety' coaches appeared on the roads in the Regency period. The basic notion of most of these designs was the correct one that the centre of gravity of the coach was too high and ought to be lowered. Other devices to prevent overturns included a small wheel fitted inside the ordinary wheel, so that if the wheel broke or came off, the coach would be supported by the smaller wheel and not come crashing down on the axle.

In 1819 a 'safety' coach named the *Sovereign* went into service on the Brighton road. It was markedly different in appearance from other coaches, being in general lower, lighter, and wider between the wheels. It carried no passengers or luggage on the roof. The outside passengers sat in an open compartment behind the box, with the luggage in a boot beneath their feet and the closed body of the coach behind them. The wheels were smaller than normal which, with greater width and lower centre of gravity, meant that if the wheels came off on one side, the coach was unlikely to topple right over. All in all it appears to have been a thoroughly sensible design and if it were true, as reported, that it did the journey in the same time as other coaches (then about six hours), it is surprising that it did not effect a permanent change in coach design, especially as it proved very popular with the travelling public and compelled other proprietors to put 'safety' coaches of their own on the road.

Within a year or two, the Brighton road was crowded with so-called 'safety' coaches. But the discerning observer would have failed to notice any difference between them and the vehicles they had supposedly displaced. All was in the name. One proprietor proudly announced that as his coach had been running for six years without an accident, it could truly be called a 'safety' coach.

In 1821 there were reports that a coach built according to one of the new designs had overturned, though they were denied by the proprietor who said that it had merely 'reclined' against a bank. Like many other bright ideas in coach design, the type pioneered by the *Sovereign* never caught on. Various new 'safety' coaches popped up at odd times throughout the 1820s and 1830s, but none of them realised the fond hopes of its inventor in effecting a revolution in the coachbuilding trade.

The Post Office was besieged with novel schemes for moving the mail with greater speed and efficiency. Some of the ideas advanced were sensible and might well have been carried out if it had not been for the great expense involved in rebuilding all the mail coaches. Some were ingenious but impracticable, and some were merely dotty. A military gentleman advocated firing the mail in shells from stage to stage; a good bombardier, he said, could hit a target three miles away to within a few feet. Someone else wanted to build a tube, along which a box containing the mail bags would be impelled by steam pressure. A Mr Slade said he could shift the mail at a speed of sixty miles an hour but, although he had calculated the cost – two thousand pounds a mile – he did not explain how it was to be done; nor did the Post Office trouble to inquire. Rather more interest was shown in various forms of steam engine: a mail railway was suggested before George Stephenson took out his first patent, though the Post Office felt that steam-driven road vehicles held greater promise. In the end, of course, the Post Office adopted no innovations; the railway companies did the job instead.

Allowing for the numerous coaching journeys that passed without incident and therefore without report, the impression remains that those who travelled frequently by coach were likely to find themselves at some time catapulted into a hedge or otherwise knocked about. But the chances of being maimed or killed were small. The majority of upsets and overturns resulted in nothing worse than torn clothing, bruised limbs and brief attacks of hysterics. Devotees of coaching cited the mild results of coaching accidents as an advantage over the – to their way of thinking – far more dangerous railways. "You get upset in a coach and there you are. You get upset in a railway and where are you?" An unanswerable question.

Even if safety could be guaranteed, not everyone regarded the prospect of a journey by coach as a pleasant one. John Byng, writing admittedly before the palmy days of coaching, expressed his delight in walking or riding ("on a tolerable horse") but considered that being "box'd up in a stinking coach, dependent on the hours and guidance of others, submitting to miserable associates, and obliged to hear their nonsense, is great wretchedness".

Judging from contemporary fiction, and indeed some true accounts as well, the passengers in an eighteenth-century stage-coach seem to have formed a standard social group. A high proportion appear to have been seriously over-weight. There was frequently a military gentleman, or one posing as such whose true character was revealed as decidedly unmilitary when a highwayman held up the coach. There was always at least one stout matron and a young woman of either hysterical disposition or questionable moral character, perhaps both. There was usually a coarse and drunken farmer, like those Karl Philipp Moritz travelled with from Northampton to London, and a mild and nervous professional gentleman – typically a lawyer. A splendid group-portrait of a not dissimilar American coachload appeared in John Ford's film *Stage-Coach*, while the disagreeable aspects of travelling with such a heterogeneous group on the Chester road at the beginning of the eighteenth century were never described better than in a verse attributed to Dean Swift.

Roused from sound sleep – thrice called – at length I rise,
Yawning, stretch out my arms, half closed my eyes;

By steps and langthorn enter the machine,
And take my place, how cordially, between
Two aged matrons of excessive bulk,
To mend the matter, too, of meaner folk;
While in like mood, jammed in on t'other side,
A bullying captain and a fair one ride,
Foolish as fair, and in whose lap a boy –
Our plague eternal, but *her* only joy.
At last, the glorious number to complete,
Steps in my landlord for that bodkin seat;
When soon, by every hillock, rut, and stone,
In each other's faces by turns we're thrown.
This grandam scolds, *that* coughs, the captain swears,
The fair one screams, and has a thousand fears;
While our plump landlord, trained in other lore,
Slumbers at ease, nor yet ashamed to snore;
And Master Dicky, in his mother's lap,
Squalling, at once brings up three meals of pap.
Sweet company! Next time, I do protest, Sir,
I'd walk to Dublin, ere I ride to Chester.

The thought of being thrust into close proximity with strangers for hours on end must have deprived the stage-coaches of many potential fares. It was one of the chief reasons why some people hired a postchaise, though at three times the cost and with little improvement in time. In the early years of coaching, it was not unknown for some wealthy traveller to hire the whole coach, in order to acquire veto rights over his or her travelling companions. Very fat people often hired two seats to save both themselves and their fellow-passengers from being crushed, though this sensible, if expensive, expedient did not always succeed in its purpose. One corpulent gentleman, having sent his servant to buy his two seats, arrived at the coach office to find he had one seat inside and the other outside.

The British people had not then learned the virtue, if it is a virtue, of ignoring as far as possible the existence of other passengers on a public vehicle. Crammed shoulder to shoulder and knee to knee inside a coach, there was no easy escape from a bore, a drunk, or for that matter a lecher, although lechers were not often a problem. Women seem to have frequently travelled alone, and less nervously than they did in a later age; there was a certain chivalry on the road, and male travellers would often pay for women's meals (women then were, of course, seldom earners) as an ordinary matter of politeness.

Some people, then as now, were adept at defending themselves against attempts to involve them in conversation. William Blew quotes the following exchange, printed in *The Sussex Advertiser* in March 1800.

A few days ago two persons, strangers to each other, took their departure together in one of the public carriages. After some time one of them said, "Here is a fine morning, sir". The other remained silent. They rolled on a mile or two, when the first spoke again, "Well, how do you do now, sir?" "I am very well, thank you, sir," was the answer, but no more. Some time afterwards the talkative gentleman accosted his silent companion with, "Well, my friend, and how are you now?" "I am as well", was the reply, "as when you asked me before, and if I ail anything I will let you know."

The response seems a trifle curmudgeonly. For two gentlemen sitting opposite each other to exchange no word throughout the journey is carrying reticence rather far. A less offensive method of discouraging conversation was that of the deaf man at the Pig and Crossbow, where Mr Jorrocks witnessed this exchange: "'You find it very warm inside, I should think, sir?' 'Thank ye, thank ye, my good friend; I'm rayther deaf, but I presume you're inquiring after my wife and daughters – they are very well, I thank ye.' 'Where will you sit at dinner?' rejoins the first speaker. . . . 'It is two years since I saw him'. 'No; where will you sit, sir? I said'. 'Oh, John? I beg your pardon – I'm rayther deaf – he's in Jamaica with his regiment'. . . .".

That fastidious actor, William Macready, on his way to London from Birmingham not long after his first success as a seventeen-year-old Romeo, travelled with hope but without enjoyment. "I got into the coach; its odours were many, various, and unpleasantly mingled, and the passengers, a half-drunken sailor and an old woman, did not impress me with the prospect of a very pleasant journey."

Half-drunken sailors and old women were to be expected. Some unfortunate travellers put up with far stranger companions. Leslie Gardiner repeats a charming if unlikely story of a gentleman who boarded a night coach and, when dawn came, discovered that the fur-coated gentleman he had been chatting to was a performing bear. Two ladies joining the Norwich coach at

Chelmsford were told that the only seats were inside, where there was already one other lady. She, unfortunately, had died on the road an hour or so before. Unwilling to walk, the two women climbed gingerly on board and rode the rest of the journey opposite the steadily stiffening corpse.

Corpses at least are harmless. Some travellers were not. A coachman on the Brighton-Portsmouth road was startled one day to hear screams coming from inside, where the only passengers were a man, a woman, and her small daughter. Stopping the coach to investigate, he found that the man was biting the woman with great violence. It turned out, though, that the man was the woman's husband, and for some strange reason this made everyone feel better about the incident.

A stage-coach traveller might be spared both corpses and lunatics only to find himself among dangerous criminals. As Pip says in *Great Expectations*, it was customary to carry convicts by coach, and he had "more than once seen them on the high road dangling their ironed legs over the coach roof". One of them sat behind him on the coach down from London, "with his breath on the hair of my head". In 1779 John Wesley rode in a coach with ten convicts, all apparently travelling in the basket behind and understandably, though to the distress of the great preacher, "loudly blaspheming".

Although convicts were naturally accompanied by an armed guard, it was perhaps unwise to put as many as ten of them, chained or not, on one coach; for whatever their character before conviction, in the nineteenth century convicts soon became violent and desperate men. One day in 1829, a Chester stage-coach, otherwise empty, took on twelve convicts who were being sent south to be transported. Two keepers travelled with them. In a quiet part of the road south of Coventry, four of the convicts succeeded in overpowering the coachman and guard, who were sitting in the guard's seat at the rear, while those inside the coach grabbed the remaining keeper. The four captives were hastily bound, the convicts saying that they wished them no harm but were determined to gain their own freedom. Unfortunately, they were disturbed by the approach of another coach before they could unlock their fetters, and most of them were soon recaptured in the surrounding countryside.

TWELVE

Dragsman and Shooter

The rosy mists of nostalgia that hover about the coaching age gather thickest around that substantial person, the coachman. A large man, bulky with capes and greatcoats, his fleshy face coloured by wind and alcohol, he sits massively upon his box, the buckled reins resting easily in his left hand, the tapering whip clasped lightly in his right. Porters and stablehands look up to him, passengers approach him with diffidence, envying the one among them who is invited to take the seat of honour on the box. The coachman glances about him, favouring acquaintances with a condescending nod, says a word to the stablehand at the horses' heads, and with the slightest movement of his wrist sets his team rattling off along the road.

Popular stereotypes are misleading: coachmen were not necessarily fat and a few of them did not drink; but the image of the coachman that most people have now was already formed before the stage-coach disappeared, and it fitted many a coachman well enough. The image was firmly impressed upon the national consciousness by the best-known (though fictional) of all coachmen, Tony Weller of the Bell Savage:

> In a small room in the vicinity of the stable-yard . . . sat Mr Weller senior, preparing himself for his journey to London. He was sitting in an excellent attitude for having his portrait taken.
>
> It is very possible that at some earlier period of his career, Mr Weller's profile might have presented a bold and determined outline. His face, however, had expanded under the influence of good living, and a disposition remarkable for resignation; and its bold fleshy curves had so far extended beyond the limits originally

assigned them, that unless you took a full view of his countenance in front, it was difficult to distinguish more than the extreme tip of a very rubicund nose. His chin, from the same cause, had acquired the grave and imposing form which is generally described by prefixing the word 'double' to that expressive feature; and his complexion exhibited that peculiarly mottled combination of colours which is only to be seen in gentlemen of his profession, and in underdone roast beef. Round his neck he wore a crimson travelling shawl, which merged into his chin by such imperceptible gradations, that it was difficult to distinguish the folds of the one, from the folds of the other. Over this, he mounted a long waistcoat of a broad pink-striped patter, and over that again, a wide-skirted green coat, ornamented with large brass buttons, whereof the two which garnished the waist, were so far apart, that no man had ever beheld them both, at the same time. His hair, which was short, sleek, and black, was just visible beneath the capacious brim of a low-crowned brown hat. His legs were encased in knee-cord breeches, and painted top-boots: and a copper watch-chain, terminating in one seal, and a key of the same material, dangled loosely from his capacious waistband.

In his own time and later Dickens was criticized for his portrait of Mr Weller as a typical stage-coachman. In the first place, he was accused of pandering to the romantic notion of a coachman which had little basis in reality. Others, including Colonel Corbett, a former 'semi-professional', objected that coachmen of the Weller type belonged to an earlier age and were extinct by the time that Mr Pickwick and his friends were conducting their inquiries into the character and manners of the age (the first instalment of *The Posthumous Papers of the Pickwick Club* appeared in March 1836). But Dicken's portrait of Mr Weller agrees with other contemporary descriptions, such as that by Washington Irving in one of his English sketches. The question of Weller's authenticity is discussed by E.W. Bovill in an appendix to his informative and entertaining book, *The England of Nimrod and Surtees*, and his conclusion, with which few would argue, is that "Tony Weller was a typical stage-coachman of his day".

Nevertheless, the typical coachman of a slow, provincial stage-coach in the late eighteenth-century was a very different figure from the 'swell dragsman' who graced the box of a fashionable day-coach out of London in the 1820s and 1830s. Broadly speaking, coachmen improved as the roads and the coaches themselves improved. The old-fashioned coachman had to drive an illmatched and overworked team drawing a heavy and cumbersome coach over rough and dangerous roads. Jolted unmercifully on his unsprung box for hours on end and in all weathers, treating his whip as a throttle (some carried six spare tips in their buttonhole), he was a hard character, who could hardly be blamed for allaying the discomforts of his job with excessive and continuous drinking. Stopping frequently at wayside inns, where he seldom had to buy his own drinks because of the value to the inn-keeper of the custom he brought, the old coachman covered his ground in an alcoholic haze. Undesirable as that might be, it was less dangerous on a slow coach, proceeding at five or six miles an hour, than on a fast coach doing twice the speed.

As his coach often required six horses to get it along at all, the old coachman knew little or nothing of the art of four-in-hand driving as it was later practised. He had no time nor inclination for smartness, swathing himself in filthy old shawls and wrapping straw around his legs. He commanded little respect from his employers and not much from those with whom he had dealings along the road; as a result, he showed equally little respect to his passengers, whose failure to tip him sufficiently might provoke, at the least, some very coarse comment on their character and family background.

Nothing could be less like the crack coachman of the 1830s. Gone were the old shawls and scarves, the bulky 'benjamin' with its layers of cloth over the shoulders and arms, the old wide-brimmed hat dusty and sweat-stained. Gone was the coarse, boozy hulk of a man with his loutish manners and his loud canvassing for tips. In his place sat a figure of considerable elegance, sporting a well-brushed white topper, the best linen, a well-cut frock coat with a posy in the buttonhole and decorated with pearl buttons. No thick-thonged 'tommy', with which his predecessor had flogged onward the tired wheelers, soiled his clean gloves; indeed, his silver-mounted whip (a present from an aristocratic patron) was not much in use, though he was capable, so his admirers said, of picking a fly off the ear of his nearside leader, if necessary. This man was an 'artist', who managed his team with skill and aplomb, threading a way through a crowded street or turning a sharp corner without reducing the brisk trot that carried his fortunate passengers forward at ten or eleven miles an hour. He disdained the tankard of beer or slug of gin, preferring a glass of sherry or Moselle. He did not strut among his passengers at the inn, loudly insisting that they 'remember the coachman', but merely remarked that this was as far as he went, and accepted graciously but undemonstratively the money slipped into his hand by his grateful clients.

These were the two extremes, and no doubt many coachmen could have been found to fit each type. The change first became apparent in the first decade of the nineteenth century, partly as a result of the general improvements in coaching typified by the success of the mails, and partly by the new interest being shown in coaching at that time by the gentry. Once, gentlemen had sneered at the coach, regarding it as effeminate or vulgar. No longer: the intricacies of driving four-in-hand were seen to be worthy of study, and the first amateur driving club was founded in 1807. At about the same time, De Quincey and his contemporaries were discovering the "glory of motion" on the mails. Not for the only time, the gentry became interested in what had hitherto been almost exclusively a middle-class activity, and although aristocratic coachmen were rare before the 1820s, upper-class influence was having some effect on stage-coaching in general a decade and more earlier than that.

Coachmen, like other people, were moulded by the society they kept, and in the nineteenth century their box-seat passengers were often men of some standing. "Masters of colleges, Professors, Tutors, Fellows, frequently sat beside me", wrote Thomas Cross of his days driving a Cambridge coach, "Church dignitaries – nay, even a Bishop I have had on the box. Indeed, were I to enumerate all the men of distinction who honoured me with their company, I should include every degree of rank in the nobility – Cabinet Ministers of both parties . . . Members of Parliament, Baronets and Squires, Clergy and Gentry, Generals and Admirals . . .". Of this exalted company, however, the only famous name he mentions is that of Lord William Bentinck, and he "was not very loquacious, his conversation being principally confined to agricultural statistics"; nevertheless, association with all those Cambridge scholars clearly had an effect, encouraging Cross's literary endeavours which earned him the name of the 'Dragsman-Poet' (possibly the first public reading of Byron's

Don Juan took place on his coach).

The profession was not, of course, transformed altogether nor in a moment. Just as there were no doubt many eighteenth-century coachmen who were neither fat nor brutal, there were many coachmen of the old type still flourishing in the 1830s and later. Mr Weller himself, though more amiable than most, was a coachman of the older type; he did not drive a crack coach, and was probably a more typical figure than the sophisticated coachman on the Brighton road who changed his buttonhole before the return journey and expected as a matter of course that the box-seat passengers would tip him half a sovereign for the privilege of riding with him.

For some passengers, the new 'flash men' were no improvement on the less cultivated coachmen of earlier times. They could be equally insolent to their poorer passengers and, finding themselves patronized by sporting gentlemen, were sometimes inclined to look down on lesser mortals as scarcely worthy of a seat on their coach. One of their fiercest critics was George Borrow (in *Romany Rye*), who must have suffered from some particularly supercilious coachmen. They were, he says,

low fellows, but masters at driving; driving was in fashion, and sprigs of nobility used to dress as coachmen, and imitate the slang and behaviour of the coachmen. . . . [They] would smoke cigars and drink sherry with the coachmen in bar-rooms and on the road; and when bidding them farewell would give them a guinea or a half-guinea, and shake them by the hand, so that these fellows, being low fellows, very naturally thought no small liquor of themselves, but would talk familiarly of their friends Lords So-and-so, the Honourable Mister So-and-so, and Sir Harry and Sir Charles, and be wonderfully saucy to any one who was not a lord or something of the kind; and this high opinion of themselves received daily augmentation from the servile homage paid them by the generality of the untitled male passengers, especially those on the forepart of the coach, who used to contend for the honour of sitting on the box with the coachman . . . As the insolence of these knights was so vast, so was their rapacity enormous; they had been so long accustomed to have crowns and half-crowns rained upon them by their admirers and flatterers that they would look at a shilling, for which many an honest labourer was happy to toil for ten hours under a broiling sun, with the utmost contempt; would blow upon it derisively or fillip it into the air before they pocketed it. . . .

This snobbery and greed is certainly not at all pleasant, but perhaps not very surprising, and it hardly seems adequate grounds for Borrow's cry of "thank Heaven! . . . that they and their vehicles have disappeared from the roads". His criticism, nevertheless, balances the rather glowing accounts of coachmen to be found in the old coaching literature, much of which was written by the kind of people Borrow disliked – gentlemen who patronized the coachmen and sometimes took their place on the box, and therefore tended to adopt a too favourable view of individual members of the trade they so much admired. Lord William Pitt Lennox's description of that fashionable dragsman, 'Parson' Dennis (said to have been once a Berkshire vicar), is one of amused tolerance, but it is not hard to imagine that the pretentious Dennis could appear in a very unattractive character to a passenger who did not happen to be the son of a duke.

> I found myself seated by one of the smartest men I ever met with at that period on the road. There was an air of conceit about him that was truly amusing, and it was rendered doubly so by his affected style of conversation. Unlike other dragsmen, he was dressed in the plainest style imaginable – a well-brushed black beaver hat, glossier than silk; a brown cutaway coat, dark Oxford mixed overalls [leggings], highly-polished Wellington boots, and fawn-coloured double kid gloves. The first object of my new companion was to inform me that he was well born, that he had been educated at Oxford, and that he was the most popular man at Bath; indeed, so much so that he was called the Beau Nash of the road. . . . During the last stage he begged that I would accept a pinch of the best Petersham mixture, informing me that it was a present from the noble Lord of that name. . . . Upon reaching [Bath] and driving up to the "York House", Mr Dennis, with the air of Louis le Grand, politely took off his hat, wished me good evening, thanked me for my gratuity, and said that if I mentioned his name at the hotel every attention would be paid to me.

Coarse or conceited, supercilious or servile, the coachman was a commanding figure at the London innyards and along the road. His performance was watched by admiring eyes. Some said they could tell a coachman's quality by the way in which he took hold of the reins and mounted the box. "In nothing", says Nimrod, "short of the higher accomplishments of our nature, is a certain propriety and neatness more required than in handling the reins and whip from a coach box".

Stablehands longed for the day when the coachman would address them by their first names, perhaps even touch his hat to them; as it was, they were delighted if he granted them a nod of recognition. Barmaids and serving girls giggled and blushed when the coachman flirted with them – as he usually did, for coachmen were well-known for their partiality to 'a nice bit of muslin' and seldom lost an opportunity to reinforce this reputation. "Wy it is that long-stage coachmen", said Mr Weller, "is alvays looked up to – a-dored I may say – by every young 'ooman in every town he vurks through, I don't know. I only know that so it is. It's a reg'lation of natur – a dispensary, as your poor mother-in-law used to say."

'Black Will' (there is doubt about his surname; it was either Bowers or Walters), who drove a coach between Oxford and London, spent three nights at Oxford and four in the capital and kept a wife in each place, neither of them aware of the other's existence. When at last the truth came out, no one seems to have been unduly upset; and if he had been tried for bigamy, it was said, no jury could have been found in Oxford to convict him.

There were exceptions to this rule as to every other, and the most memorable of them was Joe Walton, a tall, powerful man and a first-rate coachman by repute, who drove a succession of coaches on the Cambridge road. He was not a sociable man at any time, but he had a particular dislike for women. It was with the greatest distaste that he exchanged conversation with them on the subject of their luggage (of which they always had too much), but he was forced to do it because his coach carried no guard.

On the Cambridge *Star*, Joe Walton used to do the return journey of 110 miles in ten hours, including stops. He did not like to stop at all, and once refused to do so for a passenger whose hat had blown off. The passenger thereupon knocked off Joe's hat, and for that he did stop; but to take such a liberty with Joe Walton, whatever the motive, was decidedly bold, and it can be inferred that the passenger was a muscular fellow.

If he were behind time, Walton would not always stop to pick up a fare on the road. A gentleman who hailed him one day did succeed in stopping the coach, but when he did not mount quickly enough for Joe's liking, off went the coach and left him standing. But in spite of such autocratic behaviour, or perhaps because of it, Joe Walton was greatly admired. He is reported to have twice upset the *Star*, but was nevertheless regarded as very safe, as well as very fast, and he had a certain grim, sardonic humour that appealed to the young Cambridge men who often travelled on his coach. "Come, come", he would say when his nearside wheeler attempted to bolt in the direction of a pub, "I didn't know your friends lived *there*", and with a couple of punitive slashes of the whip, "Now you are got into this coach you must give up low company."

Joe Walton's short temper may have been mostly façade, a device to keep the public at a distance (there was an Oxford coachman called Spooner who, after a passenger had complained about him, refused to speak a word to any passenger thereafter). A hasty temper was a dangerous fault in the temperament of a coachman. "No man", says Lord William Pitt Lennox, "can excell on the box who is not gifted with a good temper and patience; for not only his comfort, but his life and the necks of his friends depend upon the above qualities". Horses were as capricious as coachmen and inclined to imitate their drivers, much as pet dogs acquire the characteristics of their owners. A volatile coachman meant an unpredictable team.

There was more to driving a four-in-hand coach than sitting on the box and guiding the horses along the road. The coachman had to be aware of what each horse was doing, to pick out a slack wheeler or check an over-eager leader without disturbing the rest of the team. He had to understand how the harness was put together so that he could tell when a trace was too tight or a collar too loose. He had to judge when to give his horses their heads on a slope and when to hold them up. He had to be able to judge the speed he was doing, something especially difficult at night when the passing scenery was invisible, and to take advantage of a good stretch of road to make up his time.

"Driving, sir", said Bob Pointer to one of the undergraduates who eagerly shared his box on the Oxford road, "is very like life; it's all so smooth when you start with the best team, so well-behaved and handsome; but get on a bit, and you will find you have some hills to go up and down, with all sorts of horses, as they used to give us over the middle ground". Many a young gentleman learned his driving from Bob Pointer and his colleagues, and first handled the 'ribbons' under their amiable and

31. A mail-coach stuck in the snow, after Pollard, 1825. The guard has taken one of the leaders and rides off with the mail, leaving coachman and passengers to extricate themselves as best they may.

32. Mail-coaches passing in the night.

33. An old ostler propping up the stable door. A large number of people, besides coachmen, depended for their livelihood on the coaching business.

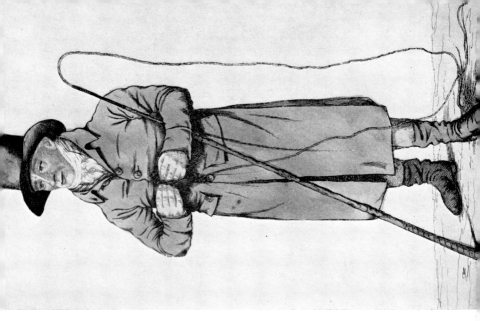

34. (*Left*) the picture of elegance: a fashionable coachman of the 1830s, after H. Alken.

35. (*Right*) Dick Vaughan, "Hell-fire Dick", of the Cambridge "Telegraph". Renowned as a fine judge of horses and a dashing coachman, he was eventually killed in an accident.

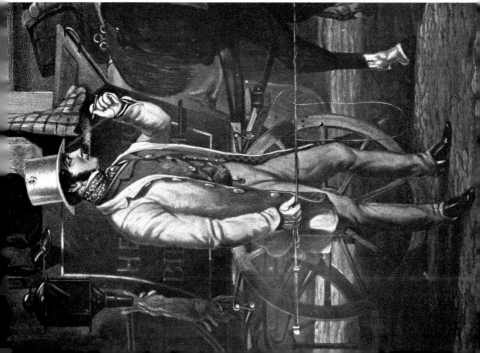

36. The yard of the Bell Savage.

37. Gurney's steam carriage on the Bath Road. The publication of splendid prints of steam carriages in calm and capable progress has helped to create a slightly misleading impression of their actual performance.

38. Hancock's "Enterprise" carrying passengers between Paddington and the City in 1833. Many people must have thought road carriages a better bet than locomotives in the dawning age of steam, especially as some of the toughest teething problems of the railways were concerned with the actual rails rather than the locomotives.

39. Like defeated nations accepting post-war aid from their conquerors, coaches and carriages in the early railway age were frequently carried by train for the greater part of their journey.

40. "The End of the Manchester 'Defiance'." A touching memorial to a vanishing age—the once-proud stage-coach in use as a hen coop, and a train chugging by in the distance.

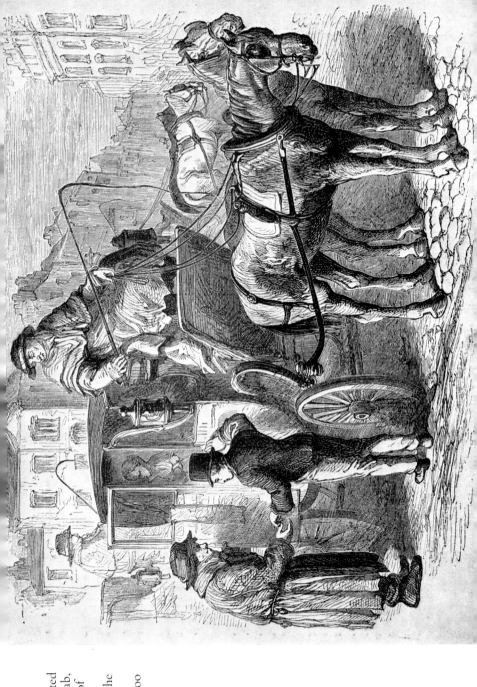

41. A private coach converted to serve as a cab, from a print of 1866. The condition of the horses was probably all too typical.

42. A model of the original "Omnibus", in the Science Museum, London.

43. The St Albans and Barnet coach. Coaching began to be "revived" (like steam locomotives) before it had disappeared, and the revival has continued sporadically ever since.

expert guidance. "And another thing, sir", Bob Pointer would say, "never let your horses know you are driving them, or, like women, they may get restive. Don't pull and haul, and stick your elbows a-kimbo; keep your hands as though you were playing the piano; let every horse be at work, and don't get flurried; handle their mouths lightly; do all this, and you might even drive four young ladies without ever rustling their feathers or their tempers".

The purely technical aspects of driving a coach and four could be (and were) endlessly discussed; the instructions contained in one of the old driving manuals inspire feelings of gratitude for the comparative simplicity of the motor vehicle. Turning a corner, for instance: there was much more to it than applying the brake and turning the steering wheel. It was necessary to make the wheelers follow the leaders in an unbroken arc, and to prevent their inclination to make their own turn too soon, for, according to the Duke of Beaufort, "wheel-horses that have been much driven get very cunning, and they feel the office given to the leaders by the rein which runs alongside of their heads". The leaders first had to be 'pointed' into the turn, then (for a right-hand turn) the nearside wheeler had to be held back slightly and the offside wheeler urged on, so as to keep the pole between the leaders (by analogy with the wheels of a car making the same manoeuvre, this is the opposite of what would be expected, but horses are animals, not machines). In coaching language, 'point your leaders and shoot your wheelers' was the term to describe the cornering manoeuvre. It was equally important to make full use of the space available; too sharp a turn and the coach tended to 'go on' or, at worst, go over. But if the turn was taken too early, the coach would cut across the corner, slipping off the road or striking a verge, perhaps with disastrous results.

"The requisites for driving", wrote Lord Algernon St Maur, "are good eyes, strong arms, light hands, good nerves, good temper, and plenty of practice." Obviously, it was a great advantage to know the road, and that is one good reason why coachmen generally stuck to the same road year after year. They got to know their ground and the temperaments of the horses and, allowing for varying conditions, followed a precise routine rather as a racing driver knows every inch of the course and accelerates, brakes, and changes gear at exactly the same spot on

each circuit of the track. When Nimrod on one occasion offered
to stand in for a stage-coachman, he was given detailed advice by
the man he was replacing:

> That middle twelve miles of ground is a punisher, and you must
> mind what you are at with this load. You have two hills to go down
> and three to go up in the first seven miles. Don't stop to put the
> chain on, as they'll hold well, and the tackle is good; and don't let
> them walk up the hills, for they are bad hands at that; you will lose a
> horse's draught by it, and perhaps get hung up on one of them. You
> must take fifty minutes to do the first seven miles, and good work
> too. When you get to the top of the last hill, get down and put your
> near leader to the cheek, and they'll toddle you over the last five
> miles in half an hour with all the pleasure alive.

The expertise displayed by various coachmen was eagerly
discussed and criticized in a manner comparable with games-
players today. Some coachmen were admired for particular
virtues – their ability to keep time with inferior 'cattle' or their
skill at negotiating a particularly tricky piece of road – just as a
tennis player may be admired for his service or his lobbing. The
quality of a tennis player, still more a cricketer, is usually
immediately apparent from his style, regardless of the score in the
game. On the box too, style was a sign of excellence, and it
consisted, broadly, of a minimum of movement. "Strange as it
may appear to some", wrote Edward Corbett, "I believe one of
the best tests that can be applied to a coachman is that he should
appear to do nothing." How annoying it was for the informed
critic to see "a Johnny Raw . . . clawing at his reins and reaching
down to his knees for them". The worst horrors were perpetrated
on private carriages: "That dreadful sight", said the Duke of
Beaufort, "which is to be seen a hundred and more times every day
in the streets of London, of gentlemen and their coachmen
(gardeners, I might say) driving one or a pair with their hands
close up to their noses, and a rein in each hand, the two hands being
from six to twelve inches apart, is enough to give anyone, with the
least notion of how a man should drive, a fit of the shivers."

No less important than style or skill to the long-distance stage-
coachman was stamina. The average distance driven was about
fifty miles, but many coachmen covered twice as many miles in a
day. 'Up' coachmen changed places with 'down' coachmen if
possible, covering 'both sides of the ground' on different coaches.

Sir St Vincent Cotton changed places with Bob Brackenbury at the half-way point when Jorrocks rode the *Age* to Brighton. The London coachman on the *Wonder* went as far as Redbourn, where Harry Lilley took over until he met the 'down' coach, where the two coachmen changed places, and finally, the great Sam Hayward drove from Birmingham to Shrewsbury. Some coachmen did more than one hundred miles a day. Joe Walton drove to Cambridge and back for a good many years, and when he first did so, before the *Star* was put on, the time one way was seven hours. That performance was exceeded by a hard-working Norfolk coachman, Jack Thorogood, who for two years drove daily between Norwich and London, a distance of nearly 120 miles, without missing a day. Some men must have suffered as much from mental strain as physical fatigue. Tom Cross, driving seventy miles a day, complained, "In the morning, particularly in the winter, from bed to the box, and in the evening from the box to bed, became too wearing to suit either my inclination or my constitution. . . . I could not but consider myself a prisoner".

The demanding nature of the job may have been responsible for the career of 'Unlucky' Upfold who, after many years as a skilful and safe coachman on the Brighton–Southampton road, suddenly became horribly prone to accidents.

Upfold, who was born about 1786, drove a coach throughout the great years of coaching. For nearly thirty years, so far as is know, he never had a serious accident, but in 1831 his coach was overturned and Upfold broke a leg. Not long after he had resumed his place on the box, the coach broke an axle and again overturned, putting him out of action for a further period. A year after that, 'Unlucky' Upfold, stopped at an inn and left his horses in charge of the box-seat passenger, presumably a sensible and knowledgeable person. Taking his drink in the bar a minute or two later, Upfold was horrified to see the passenger entering the room, leaving the horses unattended. He hastened outside as fast as one of his considerable girth was able, to see the coach just moving off. In his efforts to stop the team, he received a kick that broke his leg and knocked him to the ground, where a wheel passed over his other leg and broke that too.

Some years passed without further mishap. Upfold was again driving the coach on the Brighton–Southampton road, negotiating daily the very awkward double bend on a hill east of

Worthing as he had done so often before. On the fatal day, he had a passenger, Mr Pasco of Chichester, on the box seat who later testified that Upfold was perfectly sober and driving well – until they reached the double bend. The first half of the bend was taken so badly that Mr Pasco called out in consternation, "Upfold, what are you at with the horses"? The unlucky coachman, struggling to regain control, said, "I have pulled the wrong rein". They were the last words he ever spoke. A moment later, the coach went over, pinning coachman and passenger beneath. It was thought that the coachman's great bulk protected Mr Pasco from serious injury. But poor Upfold was dead when they pulled the coach off him.

It was a hazardous trade; Upfold was not the only coachman killed on the box. Between 1834 and 1837 the deaths of half a dozen coachmen were reported: the driver of the Halifax mail died after hitting a bridge near Sheffield; the Newcastle–Carlisle mail overturned, killing the coachman; the Exeter mail was upset in a fog and the coachman killed; the Manchester *Peveril of the Peak* overturned near Bradford, falling on the coachman, who later died. It is noticeable that these accidents all concerned mail-coaches, with the single exception of a crack long-distance stage. It seems likely that other casualties occurred on less fashionable coaches.

The job was more dangerous than most, and not well-paid, although a coachman could expect to make as much from tips in one day as his week's wages, and those who drove the fast coaches on high-tipping routes like the Brighton or Cheltenham roads made considerably more. But the job had status and, as appears in numerous anecdotes, a strong sense of professional camaraderie. Proprietors naturally encouraged these inexpensive job assets, and did their bit towards promoting a sense of fellowship by giving a dinner for their coachmen once a year. The annual celebration laid on by Mrs Nelson at the Bull, Aldgate, lasted for three days so that all those out on the road should be able to attend.

Mrs Nelson treated her coachmen and guards especially well. A number of them boarded at the Bull, paying lower rates than ordinary customers while enjoying privileges denied to commercial guests. They had their beds for nothing and paid only 1s 6d for their dinner, but tipped the staff heavily, no doubt as an example to their passengers. Their dinners were formal and exclusive. According to Stanley Harris, it was their custom to address each other not as 'Dick' or 'Charlie', not even 'Mr Jones' or 'Mr Smith', but by the name of the road they worked – 'Oxford', 'Exeter', 'Norwich', etc., like characters in a Shakespearean history play.

Although guests were sometimes invited, the coachmen were very particular about whom they asked to join them at dinner. As a rule, only those who were equally adept with a team of four horses, and preferably of gentle birth too, were admitted to the coachmen's room. One who gained an invitation with neither of those qualifications, though he *was* well acquainted with the custom of the road, was Charles Dickens. "Mr Dickens, sir", said the chairman, "we knows you knows wot's wot, but can you, sir, 'andle a vip?" The novelist frankly acknowledged that handling a whip was not one of his accomplishments.

By comparison with the tremendous figure of the coachman, the guard was definitely a junior, overshadowed by the responsibilities and the prestige that attended the senior partner, overshadowed, very often, by the sheer bulk of the coachman, the Laurel to his Hardy. Yet the guard was often a substantial character himself (it is impossible to imagine Jack Goodwin being overshadowed by anybody) who was capable of taking over the reins when for some reason the coachman was absent or disabled. His job seems much less demanding for he was not constantly at work like his colleague up front; but it had its own responsibilities and its own hazards.

Having appropriated Mr Weller to stand as a typical coachman of the period, it is perhaps permissible to burgle his inimitable creator again for a portrait of a stage-coach guard. Unlike Mr Weller, he is a minor character, whose name is never revealed, but the brief description of him (in *Nicholas Nickleby*) is stamped with authenticity.

> When the guard (who was a stout old Yorkshireman) had blown himself quite out of breath, he put the horn into a little tunnel of a basket fastened to the coach-side for the purpose, and giving himself a plentiful shower of blows on the chest and shoulders, observed it was uncommon cold; after which, he demanded of every person separately whether he was going right through, and if not where he *was* going. Satisfactory replies being made to these queries, he

surmised that the roads were pretty heavy arter that fall last night, and took the liberty of asking whether any of them gentlemen carried a snuff-box. It happening that nobody did, he remarked with a mysterious air that he had heard a medical gentleman as went down to Grantham last week, say how that snuff-taking was bad for the eyes; but for his part he had never found it so, and what he said was, that everybody should speak as they found. Nobody attempting to controvert this position, he took a small brown-paper parcel out of his hat, and putting on a pair of horn spectacles (the writing being crabbed) read the direction half-a-dozen times over; having done which, he consigned the parcel to its old place, put up his spectacles again, and stared at everybody in turn. After this, he took another blow at the horn by way of refreshment; and, having now exhausted his usual topics of conversation, folded his arms as well as he could in so many coats, and falling into a solemn silence, looked carelessly at the familiar objects which met his eye on every side as the coach rolled on; the only things he seemed to care for, being horses and droves of cattle, which he scrutinised with a critical air as they were passed upon the road.

Not all stage-coaches had guards. Low though their wages were, they had to be paid, and they took up a seat that might have been filled by a passenger. As they had to be tipped as well as the coachman, though less lavishly, they represented an additional expense for the passenger as well as the proprietor. Guards were originally put on coaches to defend them against attack by highwaymen, but the mail-coach system showed that they could be useful in other ways and helped to cut down the time of a journey by performing tasks that otherwise fell on the coachman. They looked after the paperwork, such as it was, supervized the loading and unloading of parcels and luggage, hopped down to apply the drag before descending hills, helped change the horses, answered passengers' queries, and many other matters. By about 1820, the original purpose of the guard had virtually disappeared, but as stage-coaches became faster and more efficient his other duties made him increasingly useful, so that there was probably a greater proportion of guards to stage-coaches in the later period than in the days of the highwaymen.

Had the stage-coaches not disappeared when they did, legislation would undoubtedly have been introduced before long to make guards compulsory, for not only did their presence save time, it was a safeguard against accidents of a kind that tended to occur more often when the coachman worked alone. When the coachman stopped to put the drag on the rear wheel, he had to leave his horses for a few moments unattended. Usually he would give the reins to the passenger, if there were one, on the box seat. In the event of an emergency, if the horses took fright, for instance, the coachman was in no position to deal with the situation. But if he had a guard, he had no need to leave the box.

Some brave and agile feats were performed by guards in emergencies. Lord William Pitt Lennox recorded a brave act by a guard on an Oxford coach. The horses, out of control, were racing towards a tree lying across the road:

> On we went, the coachman trying in vain to check the galloping steeds, and we had got within a few yards of the critical spot, when the guard, crawling over the roof, managed somehow or other to get on the footboard, when, with a spring, he threw himself on the back of the near wheeler, and with a giant's grasp checked the horses at the very moment the leaders were about to charge the tree.
>
> Down they came, but the guard never yielded an inch, and, with the assistance of the country people nearest at hand the leaders regained their legs without the slightest damage to man, horse, coach, or harness. A subscription for our gallant preserver was got up on the spot.

Unlike the coachmen, who seldom went more than fifty miles at a stretch, the guards sometimes stayed with long-distance coaches for the whole journey. On the mails, where the duties were more onerous and the responsibility greater, the guards usually went between 100 and 150 miles, but stage-coach guards travelled farther. On one West Country coach the guard went the whole way from Plymouth to London; the guard on Nicholas Nickleby's coach to York started from London; and on the Holyhead road, many stage-coaches carried the same guard throughout. The easier existence of the guard was thus balanced by the very long hours he often worked.

Travelling these long distances with, for much of the time, no special duties to occupy him, the enterprising guard had plenty of opportunities for carrying on all sorts of business of his own up and down the road. Smuggling was no longer the major occupation it had been, but many a guard would have found it hard to explain the presence of certain articles in the boot under his feet. The Dover mail was a particularly suspect vehicle in the eyes of the Customs and Excise men.

The game laws were liberalized in the early nineteenth century, but poaching did not disappear as a result. There must have been a considerable business in game and wild fowl conducted along some roads. Landowners often complained about it but, naturally enough, documentary evidence of such activities is slight.

Some stage-coach guards expanded their income by taking part in more-or-less legitimate trades. One of the small pleasures of travel, now gradually disappearing, is to buy an article in its place of origin of better quality or at a lower price than could be obtained at home. In the early nineteenth century, prices still varied considerably in different parts of England, and a guard making a regular journey between places as much as 200 miles apart could sometimes take advantage of these discrepancies. According to Stanley Harris, guards would purchase chain-traces in the Midlands for 10d each and sell them to the coach proprietors in London for 7s 6d each; but profit on that scale have must have been unusual.

Lord Algernon St Maur was driving the 'up' Exeter mail when one of the proprietors got in at Salisbury to travel to London.

> I was just mounting the box when the guard said to me, "I don't know what to do with the calf." "Calf", I said; "what calf?" He replied, "I did not tell you before, but veal is cheap in Dorchester and dear in London, and there's a crown to be got out of that calf, only the London butchers like them alive; but now that Billy [the proprietor] is inside perhaps I had better cut its throat, as if he hears it "bah" I might get into trouble for carrying it in the hind boot." I replied, "Leave the calf alone. I will drive very steadily out of the town, and in less than twenty minutes our only inside, barring the calf, will be fast asleep".

Lord Algernon's confidence was justified, Billy dropped off, and the calf arrived in London on the hoof.

More frequently, the guard would undertake small commissions for tradesmen requiring some particular article in a hurry, or for private individuals in the same situation. Cheeses, fresh salmon, barrels of oysters and similarly delectable goods were often transported under the guard's care, but much stranger things might be found in the boot at times, not excluding stolen silver on its way to a receiver or a corpse bound for the dissecting table. Bob Brackenbury, driving a Brighton day-coach with no guard, was carrying a lady's false teeth in his waistcoat pocket when Mr Jorrocks met him on the Brighton road; their owner required them before dinnertime.

Guards would also carry messages and undertake visits to sick relatives, children at school, or other persons absent from home, to bring a first-hand report to their anxious families. Some guards had an arrangement with an editor of a provincial newspaper to provide reports of particular events in the capital. Travelling regularly between the two distant places, stage-coach guards were in a unique position and very sensibly made the most of it.

If the guard was on the whole a less glamorous figure than the coachman, his job was not without its romantic aspects. Above all, the guard blew the coach horn, and the sound of that horn ringing out through the dawn mist on an old country road stirred in many a young heart dreams of great exploits in faraway places and in many an old one happy memories of youthful adventures. (No doubt it also awakened many an irritated citizen from his well-earned slumber.) In a countryside where technological din – mechanical and electronic – was still almost unknown, the notes of the horn rang out over great distances. The eponymous hero of R.L. Stevenson's *St Ives*, struggling across country in the dark after his escape from Edinburgh castle, caught

a whiff of the highway [when] I heard very far off, over the silent country that surrounded us, the guard's horn wailing its signal to the next post-house for a change of horses. It was like the voice of the day heard in darkness, a voice of the world heard in prison, the note of a cock crowing in the mid-seas – in short, I cannot tell you what it was like, you will have to fancy it for yourself – but I could have wept to hear it.

The purpose of the horn was to give warning of the approaching coach to other road-users, toll-keepers, and those preparing to receive the coach at a wayside inn or stable, though, unfortunately, it had little effect on droves of cattle or sheep, which formed the commonest obstacle on the road. It was a straight brass horn, flared at the end and up to three feet long, but seldom longer – in spite of the protracted instruments sometimes seen fixed to the fibreglass beams of modern roadhouses along with the cardboard wagon-wheels and the plastic onions. The coach horn was not a versatile instrument, and although a few phrases could be coaxed out of it, it was not used to play tunes. In the later years of coaching, many guards forsook the old 'yard of tin' for a keyed bugle, an instrument (like its bass version, the ophicleide) now seldom seen. An ordinary bugle of military type also appears in some old prints.

On the keyed bugle, some guards could play highly elaborate tunes – Italian opera as well as English folksongs. Bill Emery, guard on a Devon coach, could also imitate the lowing of cattle so skilfully that the animals would run across the fields towards the coach as it passed by. Another guard of outstanding musical aptitude was transferred to a poor-paying coach in the hope that the entertainment he provided would attract more customers.

Mail-coach guards were not supposed to indulge in these frivolities; but the Post Office's prohibition of keyed bugles seems not to have been strictly enforced, for some mail guards did play one, at least on country roads.

Mail guards were a cut or two above their colleagues on the stage coaches. They were Post Office employees, brilliantly uniformed in scarlet and gold, and their relations with innkeepers (especially if they were not postmasters) and coachmen were somewhat equivocal. It was never quite certain who was in charge on a mail-coach. Coachman, coach and horses belonged to, or were provided by, the proprietor, but it was the guard who was in charge of the mail – a case of responsibility without power. The mail was the first priority (passengers came second), and if for some reason the coach was unable to proceed, the guard was responsible for getting the mail to its destination by whatever means were available – hiring a chaise, riding one of the coach horses or, in some circumstances, walking. The guard was expressly charged with the duty of ensuring that the mail-coach kept time and that everyone concerned with its progress did his job properly. Any irregularity was to be reported to the Post Office. That placed the mail guard in a rather difficult position: if he incurred the hostility of the coachman by reporting him for some misdemeanour, there were many ways in which the coachman could make life difficult for him. However, it was ultimately in the interests of both that the mail should keep time; personal conflicts were rare.

Until the appearance of the smart, efficient, and rapid mail-coaches, a hint of vulgarity still clung to coaching. It did not become thoroughly respectable until the improvements in roads, coaches and horses allowed coachmanship to flourish as an art in the early nineteenth century, and the gentry began to take an interest in it. The aristocratic interest took different forms. Well-to-do gentlemen with sporting inclinations had their own private coaches, with fine teams of horses, which they drove themselves. These private coaches do not come within the scope of this book and, anyway, there is something unappealing and sterile about them. As that odd and melancholy coachman, Thomas Cross, put it:

> Although the four horses were shown off to the best advantage that skill and judgment could produce, joined to a minute attention to the appointments of both carriage and harness, still there was a nakedness about the whole affair, when contrasted with that more humble, at the same time more useful, candidate for public favour – a stage-coach – they were striving their utmost to imitate. Indeed, there was something absurd in my eye in a nobleman or gentleman sitting alone on his box, behind a splendid team that required little or no driving, with no companions to share his pleasure, envy his position, or admire his skill. . . .

Not all these gentlemen became involved in public coaching though, in one way or another, many did.

Country gentlemen often arranged to horse a coach for a stage or two in their neighbourhood, and they would sometimes insist on driving their own horses at that stage. John Warde, the famous master of foxhounds, was one of the earliest gentlemen-coachmen. He sometimes drove a stage-coach on the Birmingham road, and is said to have been responsible for introducing springs to the coachman's box. He was also one of the founders of the first driving club in 1807.

It became the custom for a coachman, when he observed that his box-seat passenger was eager and well-informed, to ask if the gentleman "had his driving gloves on". If the answer was yes, the coachman would give up his place, confident of a large tip at the end of the journey – assuming they arrived: for these amateur coachmen were a danger on the road, most of them having more spirit than experience. In the later coaching years, coachmen were sometimes forbidden by their employers to give the reins to a passenger; but it seems that they frequently did, sometimes in the face of objections from other passengers who were unwilling to risk life and limb for the sake of a sporting young gentleman's entertainment.

Some young men entered more fully into the business and made a fad of it. They imitated the language and the dress of the professional coachmen, and at least one of them had his front teeth filed down so that he could spit straight. Such behaviour was sufficiently widespread to incur the mockery of satirists. A contemporary farce is said to have given offence to certain aristocratic devotees of coaching because it made fun of their appearance and affectations. The famous clown, Grimaldi, included a coaching scene in a Christmas pantomime, driving a team of hobby horses and a child's cradle, with cheeses for wheels, and aping the style of the road in gesture and utterance.

While there were some notable characters who took the business seriously and drove a coach on a fairly regular basis or, for example, when the coachman was ill, most of the pretentious young gentlemen who hovered about the inns and coachyards were probably fairly despicable: in the words of C.G. Harper, "many of these brilliant amateurs of the road ran an essentially identical career of viciousness and mad extravagance; and . . . wasted themselves and their substance in the very shady pursuits that then characterized the 'man about town'".

One of the most famous of the gentlemen-coachmen was Sir St Vincent Cotton, a young baronet who had squandered his inheritance in the customary manner of Regency bucks and became a professional stage-coach driver in order to earn his living while enjoying his sport. He did at least stick to it, unlike some others who only came out when the weather was fine, and drove the ultra-smart *Age* on the Brighton road for several years. Mr Jorrocks shared his box on his 'Ride to Brighton', and described him as

a swellish-looking young chap, in a long-backed, rough, claret-coloured benjamin, with fancy-coloured tyes, and a bunch of flowers in his button-hole — no coachman or man of fashion, as you knows, being complete without the flower. There was nothing gammonacious about the turn-out; all werry neat and 'andsome, but as plain as plain could be; there was not even a bit of Christmas at the 'orses' ears, which I observed all the other coaches had.

Sir St Vincent had the reputation of a first-rate coachman who, although "not quite so showy or graceful a whip as some of his compeers", was "a steady and safe one". He was not by nature a particularly amiable man, but very cool in a crisis. He upset his coach more than once, but the only time he sustained a serious injury he was a passenger on the box-seat while the coach was driven by a friend. Coming over Kew Bridge, more humpy then than now, the coach bore down on the horses, which broke away and eventually piled up against some iron railings, one of which ran into Sir St Vincent's thigh. Fortunately, it missed the artery, and Sir St Vincent was soon back on the box.

The Brighton road was the favourite ground of amateur coachmen, and the swank *Age*, in particular, was associated with several gentlemen besides Sir St Vincent Cotton. One of them, Sackville Gwynne, "ran through all his property, and died in Liverpool, where he was driving a cab". At an earlier period, the proprietor and coachman of the *Age* was Harry Stevenson, a gentleman respected by all, who seems to have become involved in the coaching business through a sense of genuine vocation. He was a serious (though unsuccessful) businessman, in spite of his connections with high society (he was an Old Etonian and a graduate of Cambridge University). In the late 1820s, when he was both proprietor and coachman of the *Age*, it was the most fashionable coach on the Brighton road, outclassing even the *Comet* and the *Times*. The metal mounts and fittings of the harness were plated with silver, and instead of a guard (unusual, anyway, on a Brighton day-coach), there was a manservant in livery who passed round sandwiches from a silver box, and glasses of excellent sherry.

At the age of only twenty-six, Stevenson was struck down by a sudden and fatal disease, possibly resulting from an accident. He became delirious and had to be tied down in his bed. When he grew weak, the restraining bands were removed, and he struggled to sit up, holding himself as if once more upon the box of the *Age*. "Let them go, George; I have them", he suddenly cried, then fell back exhausted and never spoke again.

The incursions of the gentry into the coaching business had effects both good and bad – as far as the ordinary middle-class passenger was concerned probably more bad than good. For the professional coachmen – at least, those on the fast coaches – aristocratic patronage was in general a decided benefit, resulting in large tips, gifts of silver-mounted whips and buckles, and more useful articles like a brace of pheasant or a salmon. Unlike the mail guards, who had sick-benefit and pension schemes, coachmen had no insurance against sickness or other ill fortune that prevented them earning their living and, to some extent, their connections with the gentry acted as substitute. The Hon. Robert Kenyon, another well-known amateur coachman, once 'sat in' for a month on behalf of a professional coachman who was ill. When the man was able to return to duty, Mr Kenyon handed over all the tips he had been assiduously pocketing during his time on the box. The future eighth Duke of Beaufort, as a young man, put one of the last coaches on the Brighton road; he owned the coach and the horses and often drove, but he handed the tips over to his regular coachman who, as he weighed eighteen stone and took up at least one passenger seat, frequently made the journey by train.

When the railways made the coachmen redundant, one or two of them were assisted by subscriptions raised by their former passengers. This was not adequate compensation for the loss of their jobs, and it certainly did not extend to the hundreds of drivers of unfashionable, slow, night coaches, or coaches on obscure provincial roads. Private charity is not generally a satisfactory substitute for public support, and much more might have been done for the old coachmen by their former patrons, who had often shared their boxes and handled their reins. No locomotive driver was going to turn to his passenger and politely inquire if he "had his driving gloves on".

THIRTEEN

Steam Rising

Long before the end of the eighteenth century, ingenious engineers were considering the possibility of a mobile steam engine. The practical difficulties were considerable and early experiments failed to achieve sufficient precision in moving parts or to develop a boiler that was both compact and strong. A French engineer, Nicholas Joseph Cugnot, produced a steam-driven vehicle in 1769, and a second version was hopefully considered by the French army as an artillery carriage; but its speed was only $2\frac{1}{4}$ m.p.h. and it kept steam up for only fifteen minutes at a time.

One of the first in England to produce a model steam locomotive was William Murdoch, who was associated with the famous firm of Boulton and Watt. One of his early models, made about 1784, was tested a few years ago and performed briskly. Murdoch was anxious to apply his ideas to road transport, and the little three-wheeled engine that puffed busily around the furniture in his house at Redruth, Cornwall, was designed to tow a small waggon. Unfortunately for him, Boulton and Watt were not greatly interested in the possibilities of steam-driven road transport. Watt, who was always rather nervous of high-pressure steam engines, was thoroughly hostile to all ideas for a steam carriage. He refused to allow one on his property and, when he let his house, he made their exclusion a condition of the lease.

The first British inventor to carry passengers by a steam locomotive was that extraordinary Cornishman, Richard Trevithick, who in 1802 patented a boiler that was installed in a carriage. The 'puffing devil' made some progress, but was hindered by frequent mechanical breakdowns and by its incapacity to keep up the pressure for more than a short period. Trevithick eventually came to the conclusion that road surfaces were too rough for steam engines, and turned his attention to rails.

Among the host of early nineteenth-century creative mechanics in Britain, several men battled for a time with the problems of steam road transport; Joseph Bramah, for example, built a carriage designed to run by steam in 1821. But all were frustrated by the same sort of problems that had made Trevithick turn to railways as the only practical method of steam locomotion.

The first reasonably successful designer of a steam road carriage was yet another West Countryman, Goldsworthy Gurney. Born in 1793, he was a member of an influential family with friends in high places – not the least of the reasons for his comparative success in getting his vehicles on the road. Gurney was influenced by Trevithick's efforts, which he witnessed as a boy, just as Trevithick in turn was influenced (more than influenced, according to Samuel Smiles) by William Murdoch.

As the inventor himself described them, Gurney's early steam vehicles were "like a coach without the horse". It is always interesting to see how traditional designs are perpetuated regardless of fundamental changes in basic character, and this tendency is especially notable in transport; for example, the method of opening the windows by a leather belt, used on coaches, was still current in railway carriages long after the Second World War. Gurney's faithful reproduction of the form of a stage-coach in his steam carriages gave the vehicles a rather incongruous appearance – though the same form appeared, with even less relevance, on early railway trains, and aspects of the old road coach (e.g. small, face-to-face compartments) are still – or were very recently – in evidence.

Engineers agree that Gurney's engine was a very sophisticated machine for the 1820s. At 100 pounds per square inch, it operated at what was then unusually high pressure. The boiler was mounted at the rear of the coach body, which had room for six passengers; ten or twelve could ride outside. The driver sat at the front, steering two pilot wheels with a lever like the helm of a ship, and the guard, transformed into a fireman, stood at the rear of the vehicle, feeding coke into the furnace and keeping an eye on the boiler. Gurney's first carriages weighed nearly four tons, but this was later greatly reduced: the Gurney steam carriage designed to run on the London-Bath road (it never went into regular service) weighed just two tons.

Although it was no longer necessary to stop every eight or ten miles for fresh horses, Gurney's steam carriages were compelled to pause just as often in order to take on fuel and to fill up the 60-gallon water tank under the coach. The vehicle that ran between Gloucester and Cheltenham in 1831 consumed 20 pounds of coke and 10 gallons of water every mile.

After Gurney, the greatest of the pioneers of steam road vehicles was Walter Hancock, born in Marlborough of humbler stock than Gurney (his father was a cabinet-maker) but an equally enterprising and perhaps more able engineer (he was responsible, incidentally, for a great advance in wheel design). Hancock's workshops in Stratford, Essex, turned out a number of steam carriages in the early 1830s.

Hancock's first real success was a great snorting vehicle called the *Infant*. He had a penchant for incongruous names, though the *Autopsy*, as he labelled a later vehicle, was not such a happy choice. The *Infant* appeared on the Brighton road in 1832. It made the journey from London in safety, though not without minor mishaps, and was said to have covered level ground at a speed of 6–8 m.p.h., reaching 13 m.p.h. downhill. There was some doubt expressed concerning the design of the *Infant*'s boiler, but Hancock had to some extent overcome the problem of shock-induced breakdowns by fitting chain transmission, which allowed the driving axle to be properly sprung.

The *Enterprise*, which appeared in 1833, was an improvement on the *Infant*; a maximum speed of 20 m.p.h. was claimed, optimistically perhaps, though Hancock's boilers were, by the standards of the time, highly efficient. Noise, heat and smoke, which passengers accustomed to horse transport found very unpleasant novelties, were, according to the proprietor, quite overcome.

Hancock's *Enterprise* was not, like Gurney's steam carriage, "a coach without a horse". It was, rather, an omnibus without a horse, resembling the vehicles put on the streets by George Shillibeer, and it carried fourteen passengers inside. It ran for a brief time between the City and Paddington, charging a shilling for a one-way trip, and appears to have performed with reasonable efficiency. That this enterprise was so short-lived was not the fault of Hancock, but of the proprietors of the company operating the service. It seems that the company intended to copy Hancock's design but, finding they were unable to make an equally efficient vehicle, ended the contract.

A number of steam carriages built by Hancock and others were to be seen, fleetingly, on the London streets and on longer routes between 1832 and 1838. One of Hancock's vehicles on the Brighton road carried a total of nearly 13,000 passengers in 1836. There were at least six steam-carriage companies in operation up and down the country, but none of them performed what could reasonably be called a regular service. Hancock's offer to carry the mail by steam carriage was politely declined by the Post Office.

The only steam carriage that seriously rivalled public horse-drawn coach services for more than a moment was one of Gurney's vehicles, which ran twice daily between Gloucester and Cheltenham in 1831 – though even that only lasted four months. One effect of the announcement of this operation was that the ordinary coach fare was slashed from 4s to 1s in order to undercut the steam carriage. Passengers described the ride as "smooth, regular, and agreeable". It took fifty minutes, an average speed of about 10 m.p.h. (faster than the stage-coach), and although it suffered from the occasional mechanical breakdown, no serious accidents occurred (the boiler, Gurney assured the public, was designed on "philosophical principles"). The vehicle in question was smaller and more efficient than Gurney's steam coach; and the passengers travelled in a van towed behind.

Gurney provided a number of these steam 'drags' to enterprising proprietors about this time. It cost £1000 to buy one of his vehicles, but wise men preferred to hire – at the rate of 6d a mile. None of them did as well as the Gloucester-Cheltenham service (which employed three vehicles). The boilers were reasonably efficient, but there were frequent minor breakdowns through steam pipes fracturing or pumps failing – indirectly the result, probably, of continual jolting on the road.

Steam carriages had a mixed reception. Opposition was by no means as widespread as opponents pretended, and many passengers expressed approval of this new method of travelling. The dominant emotion in the public at large was plain curiosity. An announcement in 1833 that a number of prominent men were to arrive at Brighton on a steam carriage (probably the *Infant*) from London .was sufficient, says William Blew, "to bring together nearly as many idlers as Brighton happened to contain". Unfortunately for the reputation of the steam engine, the eminent passengers arrived, rather late, on nothing more interesting than one of the Brighton day-coaches. A jammed piston rod had brought the steam-carriage to a halt somewhere on the road. Among the passengers were Mr Sherman of the Bull and Mouth and Mr Chaplin of the Swan with Two Necks. Presumably they were not displeased by this demonstration of the frailty of a potential rival.

Many people, however, believed that steam locomotion, whether on rail or road, was downright dangerous, and they had plenty of evidence to support their opinion. The greatest menace was, of course, a burst boiler, not a rare disaster in the early days of the railways and not unknown on the road, where it was perhaps even more dangerous because of the closer proximity of the passengers. On one of James Scott Russell's steam carriages in Scotland, the boiler burst after the carriage had hit a stone and overturned; five people were killed, putting an end to the promising steamer service between Glasgow and Paisley. In 1831 a similar accident near Glasgow, in which two children were badly hurt, is said to have been the cause of a sardonic verse:

> Instead of *journeys*, people now
> May go upon a *Gurney*,
> With steam to do the horses' work
> By power of attorney;
> Tho' with a load it may explode,
> And you may all be undone;
> And find you're going up to Heaven,
> Instead of up to London.

There was a substantial minority of the population who were thoroughly hostile to the steam-carriage — all those whose living depended in one way or another upon horse-drawn traffic. They included humble stablehands and postboys as well as rich landowners who horsed a coach and sat on a turnpike trust, and their hostility was sometimes expressed in a disconcerting manner when steam carriages puffed through country villages. Gurney himself, when travelling on his 'steam coach' from London to Bath, was attacked by a rioting mob and forced to take shelter in a friendly stableyard. His carriage was damaged by the missiles of the rioters and failed to complete its journey. Hancock was booed and hissed when he stopped to fill up his water tank. The *Enterprise*, puffing from Paddington to St Paul's, was jostled and jammed by every cabman, coachman and wagoner it encountered.

The fiercest opposition came from the turnpike men, who believed, rightly or wrongly, that steam carriages threatened their livelihood. According to Gurney, there was nothing that the turnpike men would not do in order to make his life difficult; he even accused them of sabotage when his carriage broke an axle on a suspiciously laid stretch of loose stones.

Steam carriages were blamed for damaging the roads and causing accidents by frightening horses, and on such grounds attempts were made to prosecute them as a 'public nuisance'. Evidence could certainly be quoted of horses bolting when startled by a steam carriage, and Gurney's early four-tonner would not have done the roads much good; but on the whole these complaints were exaggerated. Horses would have grown accustomed to 'puffing devils', and steam carriages probably did not harm the road any more than horse-drawn vehicles. In fact, there was something to be said for the opposite view: that the broader wheels of the steam carriage more than compensated for its greater weight and caused less wear than the sharp hooves and narrow wheels of a coach-and-four.

These rather inconclusive arguments counted for little in the end, as the turnpike trusts were armed with a weapon that the steam carriages could not resist − tolls. Wherever possible, the trusts set crippling rates of toll for steam carriages travelling on their roads. At one place in Lancashire, where the toll for a stage-coach was 4s, a 'Gurney' had to pay £2 8s, and there were many other tolls where the discrepancy was almost as large. Even where the rates were more reasonable, steam carriages paid more than any horse-drawn vehicle.

This was one of the matters considered by a parliamentary committee which debated the merits of steam carriages in 1831. The committee had been appointed largely as a result of pressure from the influential Gurney and it was on the whole favourably disposed towards the new vehicles. It recommended legislation to prevent the trusts setting unreasonably high tolls which were obviously designed to drive steam carriages off the road, but the recommendation was ignored by the House of Commons (which had, of course, authorised the tolls upon the renewal of numerous turnpike acts).

Many sensible people in the 1830s believed, correctly, that the future of public transport belonged to steam and, incorrectly, that the next generation of steam vehicles would run on roads rather than rails. The *Birmingham Advertiser* for 10th October 1833, summed up the advantages of the road over the railway: above all, steam carriages would not require the construction of a completely new network of routes with consequent destruction of property, enormous costs in construction and maintenance of rails, loss of valuable agricultural land, and inconvenience to the travelling public who would have to adapt themselves to the "limited accommodation" provided by railways. Enthusiasts for steam carriages eagerly pointed out other advantages, some of them – for instance, the assertion that they were smoother than railways – highly dubious. As late as 1838 Sir James Anderson, "the Steam Knight of Buttevant Castle", was planning to build a fleet of 400 carriages to be drawn by steam engines in Ireland. He reckoned that each would be able to carry thirty passengers at 15 m.p.h., but the scheme sank without trace (just as his planned Forth bridge (1818) would have done had it been built).

A good case could be made for the economy of steam carriages. In theory at least, they would run more cheaply than either a stage-coach or a railway engine. They were not much faster than a horse-drawn coach, but had shown they were capable of a steady 12 m.p.h. and had on occasions considerably exceeded that speed. One inventor told the parliamentary committee that he had done 35 m.p.h. in his steam carriage without blowing up; he was probably guilty of exaggeration, but the *Automaton*, the last and best of Hancock's steam carriages, is said to have done 25 m.p.h. while transporting thirty-two spectators from a cricket match. Another point made to the committee was that an increase in speed, which could reasonably be anticipated as a result of future development, involved no significant extra cost, whereas to increase the average speed of a stage-coach from, say, 8 m.p.h. to 10 required a much greater expenditure on horses. Moreover, it was obvious that the horse-drawn coach had, near enough, reached its limit in speed by 1831; but no one could say of what future steam carriages might be capable.

Steam carriages could carry more passengers than stage-coaches, and they could be operated with greater flexibility. When a stage-coach was laid up during the winter on an uneconomical route, the horses still had to be fed, but a steam carriage cost nothing while it was not working. Steam carriages were easier to manoeuvre, it was argued, and could negotiate awkward turns or slopes more easily. Hancock conducted a significant experiment on a steep road in north London one frosty day in winter, when his steam carriage ground steadily to the top of the icy hill, leaving the coach-and-four that had begun· the ascent at the same time still slithering about at the bottom, unable to advance.

Yet with all these advantages, the steam carriage failed. By 1838 it was clear that, whether or not coaches were to be superseded by railways, steam carriages would not replace either. Goldsworthy Gurney teetered towards bankruptcy. Even now, the failure seems a shade surprising.

The failure of the steam carriage was generally blamed on the hostility of turnpike men and road commissioners – in particular, on high tolls. But it seems unlikely that, even if they had been welcomed on the turnpikes, they would have become a universal transport system. After all, it was not only in Britain that steam carriages were rejected in favour of railways. Nowhere and never has the steam engine become the chief means of road transport (although it has usually managed to keep a toehold on the roads, and still has a few admirers). The trouble was that steam carriages never completely overcame their early technical problems; burst pipes, cracked pistons and broken pumps continued to plague the later versions as they had the prototypes.

There were other teething problems that were not overcome fast enough. Although steam carriages did not have to stop for a change of horses, they did have to stop for fuel and water, and it was difficult to arrange for adequate supplies of coke at the right places. It was found, for example, that Brighton coke burned much less efficiently than London coke, a fact ascribed to the use of clay retorts in the former place which produced more gas – and extracted more carbon – from the coal. No doubt this problem could have been overcome in time; it would seem to present fewer basic difficulties, even in the 1830s, than horsing a stage-coach.

Steam-carriage companies – or, at any rate, the more promising ones – had very limited success in raising capital. Speculators judged that railways were a better bet or, perhaps more likely in the case of landowners (who still provided a large proportion of the capital for industrialisation), they declined to invest in steam carriages because they disliked them. Then, too, steam carriages were undoubtedly noisy and dirty, characteristics that were more starkly evident then that at any time since, and they were not completely safe. Segregated on railways, these drawbacks were less evident. Steam carriages *did* frighten horses, and a gentleman who had been thrown in the ditch by his rearing hunter was inclined to harbour fierce feelings about the new vehicles.

In spite of the Reform Act, the governing class was still largely the landowning class, and by and large landowners did not like steam carriages. This hostility, or at least indifference, in the club, the drawing room and the hunting field, was probably decisive in spoiling the dreams of Gurney, Hancock and their rivals even before it had become obvious that *all* forms of road transport were heading for a severe and long-lasting recession.

As several writers have observed, the false dawn of the steam carriage appears as something of a comic interlude in the rolling progress of transport history, an impression heightened by the ferocious feuds in which rival inventors engaged. The Victorians, whether they were aware of it or not, had cause for relief that the mobile steam engine was confined to railways and banished from the roads. Those great iron monsters puffing smoke from their tall chimneys and chugging along at 12 m.p.h., incongruously driven by elegant gentlemen in slim trousers, tight coats and tall hats, would not have contributed to the amenities of the city streets or the country roads. Yet the inventors and engineers of the early steam carriages deserve some credit. Their work contributed to the development of railway engines and was not wholly wasted as far as roads were concerned: the *Infant* and the *Enterprise* lived on in those impressive machines, the traction engine and the steam-roller, and there have been several more recent efforts to make something of the steam carriage – efforts which have probably not ended yet. Anyway, from one point of view the success of steam on railways and its failure on roads was largely a matter of chance circumstances; and enterprising innovations in history are not necessarily uninteresting because they do not lead anywhere. Cul-de-sacs are sometimes more rewarding than throughways.

Where is the road now, and its merry incidents of life? Is there no Chelsea or Greenwich for the old honest pimple-nosed coachman? I wonder where are they, these good fellows? Is old Weller alive or dead? and the waiters, yea, and the inns at which they waited, and the cold-round-of-beefs inside, and the stunted ostler, with his blue nose and clinking pail, where is he, and where is his generation? To those great geniuses now in petticoats, who shall write novels for the beloved reader's children, these men and things will be as much legend and history as Nineveh, or Coeur-de-Lion, or Jack Sheppard. For them stage-coaches will have become romances – a team of four bays as fabulous as Bucephalus or Black Bess. Ah, how their coats shone, as the stablemen pulled their clothes off, and away they went: ah, how their tails shook, as with smoking sides at the stage's end they demurely walked away into the inn-yard. Alas! we shall never hear the horn sing at midnight, or see the pike-gates fly open any more.

So ran Thackeray's lament for coaching in *Vanity Fair*. It appeared in 1847, exactly ten years after coaching had recorded its last great year. By 1837, the decline had set in and the approaching end could be clearly seen. In the following year the receipts from tolls showed a sharp decline; the railway was opened between London and Birmingham, and the *Wonder* was taken off the road.

Railways were first envisaged solely as a means of transporting freight, competing with the canals rather than the roads, and the motive power was to be provided by horses. Part of the line was already laid between Stockton and Darlington (the first public railway) before the decision was taken to use steam locomotion. Railways had first proved themselves in the mines, and in the debate over rival methods of carriage in the 1820s, the chief argument of the advocates of rail was that costs would be reduced and prices consequently lowered, results that experience in the mines had suggested could reasonably be anticipated.

These beneficial effects would be enhanced by the greater speed of the railways. But not everyone was certain that railways would actually be faster. On the canals, steam navigation produced an average speed of six or seven miles an hour, and even that modest rate was more than the earliest tests with locomotives promised on railways. Although these speeds were steadily increased, the first railways were not fast. Sherman's *Wonder*, in a splendid though unavailing show of defiance, left London at the same time as the Birmingham train one day in 1838 and actually succeeded in reaching its destination first. But that was a performance never to be repeated: the *Wonder* was taken off soon afterwards.

Opposition to the railways was powerful and articulate. Many landowners who were opposed to steam engines on the road were equally opposed to them on railways, though their main objections now seem not only selfish but insignificant. Railways did not cause a devaluation of land as many landowners feared, rather the reverse in many cases. Nor is it easy to feel sympathetic towards those who complained that railways would spoil the hunting or turn the sheep a sooty black, or towards those who sold off strips of land at vastly inflated prices to the railway companies and demanded extra payments for damage to property. Some landowners were so hostile, or so rich, that they refused to sell their land at any price: the apparently illogical half-circle performed by the railway through Sutherland and Caithness, putting forty miles on to the line to Wick, is the result of the Duke of Portland's refusal to have his game disturbed by the daily passing of an 'infernal machine'.

Railways were naturally opposed by all those whose commercial interests they threatened, in other words those who were involved with other kinds of inland transport. Canals seemed to be in the most immediate danger, and canal companies were among the most ingenious in producing theories and figures to show that railways would be dangerous, uneconomical, anti-social and expensive. But the true motives of the canal companies were all too obvious, and their fears for their livelihood quickly proved justified: canals and rivers degenerated even more rapidly than the roads when the railways took over.

The coaching interests did not mount so thorough a campaign of anti-railway propaganda as the canal companies. Although the chief coach proprietors were powerful men with close business connections up and down the country, they made little effort to unite in opposition to the railways, perhaps because it was against their nature. Coaching society generally, it is sometimes said, failed to recognise the true extent of the railways' threat and was taken by surprise by the public's rapid desertion to the railways; but there is not much evidence that the coaching interests were more surprised than anyone else. Very few people foresaw the full achievement of the railways, and coachmasters like Chaplin and Horne were notably quick to spot which way the wind was blowing. Even Sherman of the Bull and Mouth (by now more respectably named the Queen's Hotel), who lost a large sum by his efforts to compete with the railways on northern routes, acknowledged realities in time to preserve his fortune by association with the Great Western Railway. If humbler coaching folk were less fortunate, the reason was probably not that they failed to see the necessity of involving themselves with the railways but that they were unable to do so.

While there was no concerted campaign by coaching against railways, there was no lack of hostility. It has been estimated that the number of horses at work on the roads in the 1830s was about one million (of which perhaps twenty per cent were coach horses), and the number of individuals who earned their living largely from the business, if pikemen, stablehands, corn-chandlers, waiters and so on are included, was probably not much less – anyway, a very large number in a population of less than twenty million. Coaching represented only a proportion of this huge business, but an important one.

It was widely feared that the railways, by putting an end to coaching, would cause an agricultural slump by knocking the bottom out of the market not only for horses but for fodder too. This was a very large item: horses consumed about one-third the quantity of foodstuffs consumed by people in about 1835. Widespread unemployment seemed inevitable. Advertisements and newspaper announcements bear witness to the hatred, inspired by fear, that individual coaching interests felt. One company, in order to emphasise the danger of railway travel, sarcastically volunteered to provide cemeteries at every stop on a railway line. Others poured scorn on the inconvenience and vast initial costs of railways. Coachmen on the Great North Road polished their wits on the navvies labouring in the cuttings alongside, but even their ridicule was probably born of fear as much as ignorance. People might say that the railways could never replace the old stage-coach, but it very soon became obvious that they could. The passenger on the box-seat cheerfully applauded coachey's sarcastic comments and his rude, whip-directed gestures as the coach passed the line-laying gangs, but a few months later, needing to make his journey in a hurry, or encouraged by reports of low fares, he took the train. The box-seat was empty, and the old coachman proceeded on his road in gloomy silence. A few months later, he was gone too, the horses were sold, and the coach stood neglected in a deserted innyard.

On the chief intercity routes, the railways quickly wiped out not only the coaches but also the old freight-carrying stage-wagons. Local newspapers of the 1840s were full of notices advertising the sale of horses, wagons and carriages. Some companies, like Pickford's, successfully transferred their operations to the railways; Pickford's in fact owned a private railway terminus in London for a time. Other long-distance carriers, bearing names familiar to generations of Englishmen, disappeared. The posting business was also hit hard, although the postchaise, a more flexible means of transport, did not disappear as quickly as the stage-coach, which had to run regularly or not at all. Some people still preferred to travel in private, and the railway, though less intimate than the coach and segregated into classes to match the social classes, showed signs of a dangerous approach to egalitarianism. ("Coaches", wrote Birch Reynardson in 1875, "did not usually carry . . . the class of roughs that sometimes are to be seen in these railroad days, in a third-class carriage, or in an excursion train".) Still, the great disparity in time and cost limited posting customers to a few diehards.

To the general public railway travel first appeared feasible in 1830, with the opening of the Liverpool-Manchester railway. By 1837, although coaching was feeling the pressure and a few coaches had already disappeared from some provincial routes, none of the big, long-distance London lines had been opened and coaching was still at its peak. The following year saw a sharp decline, and by 1840 the battle was virtually over. The completion of through lines to the south and west coasts and to the Midlands annihilated the coaching business almost at a stroke, and it was the suddenness of the railways' victory rather than the victory itself which caused so much hardship and bitterness. "Few people", wrote the Duke of Beaufort, "are aware of the misery caused by railways to innkeepers, coachmen, guards, postboys, ostlers, and housekeepers, as it all came to pass so suddenly." In 1843, the yard of the Bull and Mouth, less than ten years before one of the sights of London with coaches coming and going all day and half the night, was "a dismal scene", with hardly a horse in sight. The other coaching inns of the capital were equally deserted, and at Hounslow, the great staging post for all west-bound coaches, half of the old Lion Inn had been turned into a shop. Up and down the country, the coaching yards fell silent, and dust gathered on the tables at the roadside inns.

No crowds assembled to see the nightly departure of the London mails. When the last long-distance mail ran through Newcastle, in 1847, it flew the union flag at half-mast, and coachman and guard wore black mourning ribands. The last of the fast London day-coaches, the Bedford *Times*, disappeared the following year. Only one mail-coach was still operating in Edinburgh by 1850; that was the Carlisle mail, a 'unicorn' or 'pick-axe' outfit (three horses – two wheelers and one leader), with a fourth horse put-to on steep hills. One coaching company, giving notice of the termination of its service, announced the fact with a fine sense of occasion, "The horn will cease to blow. . .".

The ironwork of the coaches, pushed out of the way in some corner, grew rusty and their paintwork dull, though it would have taken many years of hard weather to wear away the forty or fifty coats of paint and lacquer that the best coachbuilders had lovingly employed. Few of the coaches survived (there appear to be no authentic stage-coaches of pre-Victorian construction in British transport museums, although there are one or two mails).

Villages that had once bustled with activity as a stream of coaches pulled in to change horses sank into country backwaters, while neighbouring villages rose from obscurity to take their place in the limelight thanks to their situation on the railway line. Who remembered Redbourn when the *Wonder* no longer stopped there for breakfast? And who would remember Crewe but for the great railway junction? Jane Welsh Carlyle, revisiting her birthplace of Haddington in 1849, found a ghost town: "It was the same street, the same houses; but so silent, dead, petrified" – though this gloomy appearance was due to the re-routing of the Great North Road as well as the decline of coaching.

The railways may have put some people out of work, but for others they provided new employment. It was not a particularly hard transition for a guard on the coaches to become a guard on the railways, and the belief among some coachmen that the railway directors deliberately avoided employing those who had been engaged in the coaching business was probably pure fiction. But while the guard might easily change from road to rail, no case is known of a coachman who became an engine-driver.

It is the coachman, partly perhaps because he was the central figure in the drama, who seems to have suffered most. One of the few true professionals among coachmen who wrote his memoirs was also one of the most bitter critics of the railways: they were "conceived in error – born in misrepresentation and falsehood – reared in malversation and fraud – and attained their present growth by monopoly and injustice", wrote Thomas Cross, emotion turning his commas into angry dashes. As he trotted north on the ever-emptier King's Lynn *Union*, he would gloomily sing, to the tune of "The Trotting Horse", a song he had written himself.

> Now, if the railroads, that vile foe, t'our sport
>   should put an end,
> And England's pride, the four-in-hand, no longer
>   have a friend,
> To some lone cot I will retire, and dream upon the past,
> And live again on what was once the fastest of the fast.

In fact, he did not retire to his lone cot for some time; he was preserved from hopeless poverty by the patronage of an amiable East Anglian squire, and spent his last years in a home for distressed gentlefolk.

Other cases of coachmen being rescued by the charity of their former customers were recorded. Cross himself mentions Francis Faulkner of the Portsmouth *Rocket*, who retired on an annuity bought through a subscription raised by his well-to-do passengers. (There is a Francis Faulkner buried, according to C.G. Harper, in a churchyard not far from Portsmouth, who is said to have been a guard on the *Rocket* – it must be the same man. His last request, was that coaches passing by his burial place should sound their horns when they drew near his grave: according to tradition, this request was faithfully fulfilled.) The Duke of Beaufort, an enthusiastic amateur, took several former coachmen into his household. Harry Simpson, who had driven the *Quicksilver* Devonport mail at one time, found a welcome in the coach house of a prosperous Welsh baronet, who put up with Harry's surly ways and sharp remarks for the sake of old times. There are stories, true or false, of gentlemen alighting from trains and recognizing in the stooped and shabby figure doing some light portering about the yard the wreck of old George who used to drive the *Telegraph*, and whisking him away to a contented retirement.

Nowadays, presumably, some kind of government action would be taken to prevent hardship for the people put out of work by such a drastic change. But the numerous petitions to parliament from coach proprietors, and even individual coachmen, in the 1830s and 1840s were ignored. Something might have been done, even within the political conventions of that time. Very large sums had been paid in compensation to slave-owners when slavery was abolished, and in view of the government's favourable treatment of the railway companies, the neglect of their outmoded rivals was shameful.

Thackeray was not the only one who wondered where the old coachmen had gone. They seemed to disappear quite suddenly, like the coaches. Colonel Corbett concluded that "the larger part died off rapidly. They were never a long-lived class of men". Some of them, however, are known to have lived to a great age. Thomas Cross, in spite of chronic misanthropy, reached eighty-six, and the number of elderly fellows who turned up in the late nineteenth or early twentieth century, each claiming to be "the last of the old coachmen", is very considerable. (Leslie Gardiner talked in 1960 to an old man at Laggan who had driven the mail from Kingussie to Fort William in a coach-and-four – a service that continued well into the twentieth century).

Some coachmen, discarding dignity, found work on local vehicles, which increased in number to deal with the traffic to and from the railway stations. A figure once familiar on the open road could sometimes be seen driving a city omnibus, a hard transition for a four-in-hand coachman, as if a jet fighter pilot were to take the wheel of a motor bus. No wonder the old coachmen looked glum and waxed garrulous on the subject of the superiority of the old days, "afore rails and reform turned everything upside down".

Joe Walton, once the imperious coachman of the Cambridge *Star*, became a bank messenger; Jack Peers of the Southampton *Telegraph* was rescued from a workhouse. Several coachmen are known to have become landlords of inns, one of the few alternative professions that seem suitable but one that usually required some capital outlay (unless, like Tony Weller, they were lucky enough to marry a landlord's widow), and one that, like coaching, went into decline with the coming of railways. But there must have been many who were steadily ground out of a livelihood, declining from a crack Royal Mail to a provincial stage-coach, to a pair-horse short-stage, to nothing at all. "No employment being offered them by those who had taken away their very means of existence, many were driven to the most abject poverty, and some few, in despair, committed suicide." This may be too black a picture, for although the suicide of at least two ex-coachmen is recorded, the blame in neither case can be laid squarely at the railway's footplate. Little Dick Vickers, once of the Holyhead mail, hanged himself after going bankrupt as a farmer; Charlie Holmes, who had driven and horsed the *Old Blenheim*, drowned in the Thames after jumping from a boat.

Like old soldiers, the old coachmen just faded away. Perhaps there were many like Harry Littler, the story of whose end is repeated by C.G. Harper in the preface to his history of coaching:

> "Hang up my old whip over the fireplace", said Harry Littler, of the Southampton *Telegraph*, when the London and Southampton Railway was opened, in 1838, – "I shan't want it never no more": and he fell ill, turned his face to the wall, and died.

The rapidity of the railway takeover was in some part illusory. The period of three or four years which saw coaching swept from the height of its achievement was not really long enough for a complete transformation of the ways in which people got about from one place to another. What happened in that short and eventful period was that the crack long-distance coaches, including the mails, and most coaches between London and the chief provincial centres, disappeared. The short-stages lasted much longer – until suburban railway networks were built – and so did many cross-country stage-coaches. Some parts of Britain remained rail-less until quite late in the century and there local coachmasters were as busy as ever thirty of forty years after the yards of the Bull and Mouth and the Bell Savage had grown silent. What happened in London, the Midlands, and the South-east in about 1840 did not happen in Cornwall or parts of Wales until about 1880. Some coachmen who had once driven fast coaches in and out of London on the Holyhead road or the Bath road retreated into the provinces, carrying out a tactical retreat in face of the advancing rails, and a man who had in the 1830s strutted the great London coachyards found himself ten years later working some winding, cross-country road in the south-west. As the rails crept nearer and business fell, he could retreat still farther, perhaps ending on a mountainous road in North Wales or the Scottish Highlands.

Tom Cross, who stayed on the box of his ever shabbier coach during the declining years of coaching in East Anglia, left a vivid description of those sad days:

> On approaching the inn, not a solitary person did I see. The dingy, half-washed coach stood by itself outside the gates, like a deserted ship; inside the yard there was a dim, dirty place set aside for the office; in it glimmered one poor mutton candle, stuck on a piece of rusty tin, that had served the ostler for a candlestick for years; by its light I entered, and could just perceive a lantern-jawed, melancholy-looking man, whose visage indicated – indeed, seemed already to anticipate – the fate that awaited both him and me, leaning with his head upon his hand, inert and heedless, as must men who have nothing to do – this was the porter. On the other side of the counter, behind an old worm-eaten desk, sat the book-keeper. The usual salutation having passed between us, I took from the desk a long sheet of white paper [the waybill] which, with the exception of the heading, was unsullied – not the name of a passenger or parcel was written thereon!

Coaching's sun had set; the old coachman lingered for a time in the brief twilight; but soon the darkness closed in for ever. In a

few years, a public coach was as strange a sight as a steam engine
is now. The whole splendid business was swept away by the
advancing rate of change and the stern demands of industrial
society. Most people were only too glad to travel with greater
comfort and speed on the railways, and if they spared a moment's
regret for the coach, it was in the spirit of the poet whose
unforgettable lines are quoted by Lord Algernon St Maur:

> What can escape Time's all-destroying hand?
> Where's Troy, and where's the May-pole in the Strand?

Where indeed?

The minority of people who genuinely regretted the passing of
the coaching age, other than those who lost their livelihood,
were responsible for a minor revival of coaching, mainly on the
Brighton road, which began almost before the changeover from
road to rail had taken place. The Duke of Beaufort's coach has
already been mentioned, and there were several others; but they
were short-lived and hardly more significant than the current
revival of steam on a few short and obscure railway lines.

As horse and carriage remained the sole means of private
transport until the coming of the motor car, upper-class
gentlemen retained a fashionable interest in the art of driving,
and the types of private carriage continued to proliferate,
although only a small number of enthusiasts (there had never
been many) indulged in the luxury of four-in-hand coaching
(when Birch Reynardson wanted to sell the four-horse coach that
he had built at a cost of £113 for a European tour, Tattersall's
could get only £6 for it). Interest in public coaching never quite
died, and a few 'pleasure coaches' could usually be found
operating in summertime on short routes out of London and near
seaside resorts. Predictably, there was a noticeable rise in public
interest about 1870, by which time a generation had grown up
that had not been born when the coaching age ended, and it was
this revival that encouraged several elderly 'gentlemen-
coachmen' to write down their stories of the road. Their stories
bore a certain similarity, both in content and in form. Nearly all
began, for instance, with a modest protest that they were handier
with the reins than the pen – and then proceeded to write very
well (though with a skimpy sense of organization). They paid
tactful tribute to the speed and convenience of modern means of

travel, while uniting in gentle regret for the passing of the coach and endorsing, one and all, the remark of the old coachman, that "them as have seen coaches, afore rails came into fashion, have seen something worth remembering".

BIBLIOGRAPHY

As this book is not based on original research, extensive footnotes would be otiose; but for the same reason profound debts ought to be acknowledged to the writers quoted in the text and listed below. General works and works of fiction are not included in this list.

Philip S. Bagwell, *The Transport Revolution from 1770*, Batsford, 1974

F.E. Baines, *On the Track of the Mail-Coach*, Richard Bentley, 1895

Alan Bates, *Directory of Stage-Coach Services 1836*, David and Charles, 1969

Duke of Beaufort and others, *Driving*, Longmans (Badminton Library), 1889

Anthony Bird, *Roads and Vehicles*, Longmans, 1969

William C.A. Blew, *Brighton and its Coaches: A History of the London and Brighton Road*, John C. Nimmo, 1894

E.W. Bovill, *The England of Nimrod and Surtees*, Oxford University Press, 1959

E.W. Bovill, *English Country Life 1780–1830*, Oxford University Press, 1962

Anthony Burgess, *Coaching Days of England*, Paul Elek, 1966

Charles R. Clear, *John Palmer, Mail Coach Pioneer*, Blandford, 1955

John Copeland, *Roads and their Traffic 1750–1850*, David and Charles, 1968

Edward Corbett, *An Old Coachman's Chatter*, Richard Bentley, 1890

J. Crofts, *Packhorse, Waggon and Post: Land Carriage and Communications under the Tudors and Stuarts*, Routledge, 1967

Thomas Cross, *The Autobiography of a Stage Coachman*, 2 vols, Kegan Paul, ed. 1904

Jacques Damase, *Carriages,* Weidenfeld and Nicolson, 1968

C. St. C.B. Davison, *History of Steam Road Vehicles*, Her Majesty's Stationery Office, 1953

Thomas de Quincey, *The English Mail Coach and Other Essays*, Dent (Everyman), 1912

Roy Devereux, *John Loudon McAdam: Chapters in the History of Highways*, Oxford University Press, 1936

Leslie Gardiner, *Stage-Coach to John o' Groats*, Hollis and Carter, 1961

Sir Walter Gilbey, *Early Carriages and Roads*, Vinton & Co., 1903

Ronald Good, *The Old Roads of Dorset*, (new ed.) Horace G. Commin, 1966

Elizabeth Grant, *Memoirs of a Highland Lady 1797–1827*, (rev. ed.) John Murray, 1950

J.W. Gregory, *The Story of the Road*, 2nd ed., A. and C. Black, 1938

A.R.B. Haldane, *Three Centuries of Scottish Posts: An Historical Survey to 1836*, Edinburgh University Press, 1971

Charles G. Harper, *Stage-Coach and Mail in Days of Yore*, 2 vols, Chapman and Hall, 1903

Stanley Harris, *Old Coaching Days*, Richard Bentley, 1882

Stanley Harris, *The Coaching Age*, Richard Bentley, 1885

William Hazlitt, *Selected Writings*, (ed. Ronald Blythe) Penguin, 1970

Geoffrey Hindley, *A History of Roads*, Peter Davies, 1971

James Wilson Hyde, *The Royal Mail, its Curiosities and 'Romance*, Blackwood, 1885

Washington Irving, "The Sketchbook of Geoffrey Crayon, Gent.", *Works*, 2, Putnam, New York, 1860

W.T. Jackman, *The Development of Transportation in Modern England*, (2nd ed.) Frank Cass, 1962

Alan James, *The Post*, Batsford, 1970

Michael Jamieson, *Coaching Days in the North Country*, Frank Graham, 1969

Lord William Pitt Lennox, *Coaching*, Hurst and Blackett, 1876

Hugh McCausland, *The English Carriage*, Batchworth, 1948

Captain H.E. Malet, *Annals of the Road [with] Essays on the Road, by Nimrod*, Longmans, 1876

Ethel Mann, (ed.) *An Englishman at Home and Abroad 1792–1828, being Extracts from the Diaries of J.B. Scott of Bungay, Suffolk*, Heath, Cranton, 1930

Stella Margetson, *Journey by Stages: Some Account of the People who Travelled by Stage-Coach and Mail in the Years between 1660 and 1840*, Cassell, 1967

Nimrod, *The Chace, the Road and the Turf*, (reprint) Bodley Head, 1927

Cyril Noall, *A History of Cornish Mail- and Stage-Coaches*, D. Bradford Barton, 1963

The Penny Magazine of the Society for the Diffusion of Knowledge 4, Charles Knight, 1835

William Plomer, (ed.) *Kilvert's Diary 1870–1879*, Macmillan, 1947

C.T.S. Birch Reynardson, *Down the Road, or Reminiscences of a Gentleman Coachman*, Longmans, 1875

Howard Robinson, *The British Post Office: A History*, Princeton University Press, New Jersey, 1948

Fairman Rogers, *A Manual of Coaching*, Lippincott, 1900

L.T.C. Rolt, *Thomas Telford*, Longmans, 1958

N.C. Selway, *The Regency Road: The Coaching Prints of James Pollard*, (Introduction by James Laver) Faber, 1957

Jack Simmons, (ed.) *Journeys in England*, (reprint) David and Charles, 1969

Ralph Strauss, *Carriages and Coaches: Their History and their Evolution*, Martin Secker, 1912

L.A.G. Strong, *The Rolling Road: The Story of Travel on the Roads of Britain and the Development of Public Passenger Transport*, Hutchinson, 1956

Philip Sumner, *Carriages: To the End of the Nineteenth Century*, Her Majesty's Stationery Office, 1970

László Tarr, *The History of the Carriage*, Vision, 1969

G.A. Thrupp, *The History of Coaches*, Kerby and Endean, 1877

W. Outram Tristram, *Coaching Days and Coaching Ways*, (2nd ed.) Macmillan, 1893

A.S. Turberville, (ed.) *Johnson's England*, vol. 2, Oxford University Press, 1933

Edmund Vale, *The Mail-Coach Men of the Late Eighteenth Century*, Cassell, 1960

Sidney and Beatrice Webb, *The King's Highway*, (*English Local Government* vol. 5) Longmans, 1913

Index

INDEX